At The Door of Memory

A Witness to History

AUBREY RIKE

and the
Assassination of President Kennedy

By Aubrey Rike
with Colin McSween

JFK Lancer Publications & Productions
Southlake, Texas

JFK Lancer Productions & Publications, Inc.
Southlake, Tx 76092

JFK Lancer First Edition November 2008

The goal of JFK Lancer Productions & Publications, Inc. is to make research materials concerning President John F. Kennedy easily available to everyone. Our prime concern is the accuracy and the true story of the turbulent 1960s.

For additional copies of this publication, please contact:
Email: orders@jfklancer.com
Web: www.jfklancer.com

Printed in the United States
Cover and Book Design by Sherry Fiester
Edited by Sherry Fiester

Known photographic sources are named and acknowledged where possible. The author has attempted to locate individual photographers or agencies that created or own rights to all images.

ISBN Number 0-9774657-5-6

This book is dedicated to the memory of my beloved friend Dennis "Peanuts" McGuire, and my good friend Debra Conway.

Aubrey Lee Rike
2008

Contents

Prologue

Sherry Fiester

A presidential visit to any city is always well planned; the itinerary of the president is carefully considered and security minded men consider every possible scenario for danger, carefully and skillfully planning for every contingency. The local dignitaries and press are all given special security clearance, and designated places and methods for their interaction with the president and his official entourage are carefully choreographed.

For the general public, a presidential visit is something typically experienced by watching television, or in the most opportunistic of circumstances, possibly a personal glimpse of the flagged entourage experienced as the motorcade drives past a well-maintained barricade protected by armed men whose eyes scan the crowd for signs of unrest or imminent threat.

The average American never imagines having an opportunity to relate intimately with a member of the presidential party; especially in the event of an emergency when security and vigilance is at its highest. Consequently, for the death of President Kennedy to result in affording an ordinary citizen the opportunity of rendering comfort to his surviving widow in an intimate setting is more than astounding, it suggests destiny.

Most people like to imagine that in extraordinary times, like the assassination of President Kennedy, given the opportunity they would rise to the occasion and perform exemplary tasks. However, few persons are ever afforded the opportunity to have that theory tested; Aubrey Rike and Dennis 'Peanuts'

McGuire, however, were tested. They were consigned to a complex and difficult role during an extraordinary time, and responded with emotional sensitivity and compassion. While in Trauma Room 1, Aubrey found himself at the center of an unparalleled time in history, and in doing so, assumed the unscripted yet essential role of providing selfless and heartfelt assistance to Jacqueline Kennedy.

The emotional incident Aubrey shares is at times heartbreaking, and brings unashamed tears to his eyes as he relates those private moments with Mrs. Kennedy. Now a poignant memory, Aubrey's experience also reveals some less than admirable dynamics demonstrated as the result of the death of an extraordinary leader.

Legendary American civil rights leader, Susan B. Anthony wrote:

Sooner or later, we all discover that the important moments in life are not the advertised ones; not the birthdays, the graduations, the weddings, not the great goals achieved. The real milestones are less prepossessing. They come to the door of memory.

Aubrey had a moment in time that became forever ingrained in his memory; unannounced, it came as an opportunity to offer kindness and caring to a slain President and his grieving widow. Now, he has now opened that door of memory and asked us to step through.

Sherry Fiester

Acknowledgements

From Aubrey L. Rike

Special thanks for a lifetime of encouragement and support are extended to my wife Glenda and our son, Larry. My lasting gratitude is given to those who helped me in writing this book, especially to Colin McSween who made the leap of faith and actually helped me compile my thoughts in writing. Thanks are also extended to Debra Conway, who for years asked me to put my story in book form and has now published it. My gratitude is also given to Sherry Fiester for transforming Colin's initial manuscript into my story.

Aubrey Rike, 2008

From the Publisher

Many thanks go to Jerry Dealey for last minute contributions we couldn't have gone to press without. You are our "eagle eye."

Acknowledgements

From Colin McSween

Sincere appreciation is offered to my wife Pat and our children Katie, John, Jared, Hannah, Jorin and Jaden. Without your help and support, the tedious task of transcribing, organizing and compiling a manuscript documenting Aubrey's story would have been impossible.

I would also like to acknowledge Debra Conway, Sherry Fiester and any others who helped with this work.

When writing personal memories, the story told is not always filled with documents or resources that bolster the account. To that end, I would like to thank Larry Hancock, William Law, Jerry Dealey, David S. Lifton, Jared McSween, "... Deane Gurney, Bruce and Jenny Clark, and Scott Baumann for their for their valuable assistance in providing this additional information.

Additionally, many persons generously supported me with much needed encouragement or in other practical ways. To that end, I would like to thank Beverly Oliver Massegee, Betty Windsor, Katharyn McSween, Deane Gurney, Bill and Gwen Burnett, Chuck Wade, Kenneth Holmes Jr., Don Ross, Russ Akins, Dr. Joel and Marianne Wilson, and Sonya Siltani.

My heartfelt thanks to Aubrey, my true and trusted friend; he is a real man's man, always as good as his word, patient, and kind. I will forever remember our first meeting over 17 years ago in downtown Dallas. He quietly related some of his involvements in the events following the death of President Kennedy. To be asked to assist him with his book has been an amazing experience and a most profound privilege. I will carry that honor and with me until the day that I die.

Colin McSween, 2008

Eulogy for President John F. Kennedy

Senator Mike Mansfield

On Sunday November 24, 1963, President John F. Kennedy's remains were moved from the East Room of the White House to the Rotunda of the Capitol Building to lie in state. Upon arrival of the casket members of the US Senate, the House of Representatives and the Supreme Court conducted a formal memorial ceremony. The flag draped casket was placed on Lincoln's catafalque and eulogies were read.

Senator Mike Mansfield of Montana's eulogy delivered in the Rotunda of the US Capitol ties in most fittingly with Aubrey Rike's story,

The body of President John F. Kennedy lies in repose in the East Room of the White House. November 23, 1963.

(Photographer, Abbie Rowe, National Park Service, John. F. Kennedy Library and Museum)

There was a sound of laughter; in a moment, it was no more. And so, she took a ring from her finger and placed it in his hands.

There was a wit in a man neither young nor old, but a wit full of an old man's wisdom and of a child's wisdom, and then, in a moment it was no more. And so, she took a ring from her finger and placed it in his hands.

There was a man marked with the scars of his love of country, a body active with the surge of a life far, far from spent and, in a moment, it was no more. And so, she took a ring from her finger and placed it in his hands.

There was a father with a little boy, a little girl and a joy of each in the other. In a moment, it was no more, and so she took a ring from her finger and placed it in his hands.

There was a husband who asked much and gave much, and out of the giving and the asking wove with a woman what could not be broken in life, and in a moment it was no more. And so, she took a ring from her finger and placed it in his hands, and kissed him and closed the lid of a coffin.

A piece of each of us died at that moment. Yet, in death, he gave of himself to us. He gave us of a good heart from which the laughter came. He gave us of a profound wit, from which a great leadership emerged. He gave us of a kindness and a strength fused into a human courage to seek peace without fear.

He gave us of his love that we, too, in turn, might give. He gave that we might give of ourselves, that we might give to one another until there would be no room, no room at all, for the bigotry, the hatred, prejudice, and the arrogance which converged in that moment of horror to strike him down.

In leaving us — these gifts, John Fitzgerald Kennedy, President of the United States, leaves with us. Will we take them, Mr. President? Will we have now, the sense, and the responsibility, and the courage to take them?

I pray to God that we shall and under God, we will.

At The Door of Memory

A Witness to History

AUBREY RIKE

and the
Assassination of President Kennedy

Eventually, we all discover that the important moments in life are not the advertised ones; not the birthdays, the graduations, the weddings, not the great goals achieved. The real milestones are less prepossessing. They come to the door of memory.

Susan B. Anthony

Beginnings

Chapter 1

She was one of the most beautiful women I had ever seen; but she was preoccupied with trying to somehow remove her husband's blood from the textured material of her pink suit. I handed her a wet towel and as she begin to try to find some order in the chaos surrounding her, I knew my life was forever changed.

I was born Aubrey Lee Rike on December 18, 1937, one of three boys and a girl to Lois and Jake Rike. My parents separated when I was quite young and my mother raised me, my brothers Billy and Richard, and my sister Carolyn single-handedly in Dallas, Texas. Although we had a single parent household, she managed to keep us fed, clothed and sheltered. She also instilled in us good old-fashioned values, and manners consistent with well-known southern charm.

During my early childhood a lot of people did not know how to spell or pronounce Aubrey, so using my initials they began to call me A.L. From that, my name slowly evolved from A.L. into Al. The name Al became familiar and I began introducing myself in that way; and except for a few friends and family members, I am still known as Al.

All kids dream of what they want to be when they grow up and I was no different in that way. I often thought I would like to be involved in some sort of emergency services such as a police officer, fire fighter or something similar. Even at a young age, I knew there was a great sense of accomplishment when you are able to be of assistance to someone who has been hurt or needs help. My early desire to have a job related to public service took a more narrow focus one hot summer afternoon.

Throughout my childhood, when not in school I kept myself busy playing outside with my friends. One of our favorite activities during the hotter months of the spring and summer was swimming. We would usually go to places along the Trinity River, since there were a number of places along the riverbank that were well suited for swimming. Yet, as much fun as that cooling water was, it also presented some hazards.

Like most kids, we had the "it can't happen to me" mentality. We all knew well enough that the river was home to water moccasins; we'd see them on occasion lazily sunning on the rocks near the water. Although the water moccasin is territorial, we always believed that we would be okay if we did not bother them, that they would leave us alone. Nevertheless, one day, while in the water, I was bitten on the hand.

The water moccasin is a very poisonous snake and its venom is highly toxic. I remember the burning pain, which was quickly followed by swelling that began in my hand and moved to include my entire arm. As this can be a fatal bite, I ended up in the hospital. It was a frightening injury and at one point during my ordeal, I was facing the very real possibility of amputation of my hand and possibly my arm. Thankfully, doctors managed to treat my hand successfully and I retained my arm. However, as traumatic as that event was, it confirmed my desire for a vocation in emergency services—I wanted to help others when I grew up.

I joined the United States Marine Corps in 1955 when I was 17 years of age, just before I turned 18. I was always impressed by what I had heard about the Marines and I felt that it would afford me a chance to be of service to my country. My journey as an adult began with my enlistment, and included by chance, being at Dealey Plaza. The Marines shipped all new recruits to boot camp in San Diego, California, and required us to billet overnight at what is now the Hotel Lawrence in the 300 block of South Houston Street at Dealey Plaza. A stately structure, the Hotel Lawrence was built in 1925 to serve passengers from the trains stopping at Union Station. Eight years later, being in Dealey Plaza would again begin a journey that would change my life, the assassination of President John F. Kennedy.

I went to California for my initial training and more advanced Combat Training, and finally to Alaska for 10 days of Cold Weather Training. The idea behind training in the harsh Alaska environment was to prepare us for mountainous and extreme weather combat. Warfare in cold weather is characterized not only as a battle against the enemy, but also as a battle against the elements for survival, and the United States Marine Corps wanted their soldiers who would possibly be shipped to Korea or Japan for fighting to be prepared. The Cold Weather Training certainly was appropriately named, and three days snowbound in a two-man pup tent definitely made me appreciate the warm weather in Dallas when I was home again after leaving the Marines.

Leaving Alaska, I was assigned to the 1st Marine Division, 5th Marine Regiment. I was stationed in Korea for 3 hard months in extreme conditions working a radio. I was in a TAD non-combat zone working with the removal of Marine equipment.Thankfully, I was sent back stateside to Camp Pendleton in California. While stationed at Camp Pendleton, I went to Military Police School, getting my first taste of service to others in that vocation. I found myself well suited to that type work and my experiences deepened my commitment to pursue a career related to that field.

While in California, my unit was cast as extras in two Hollywood movies. *Hold Back the Night* with John Payne, Peter Graves and Chuck Connors was about a Marine Sergeant flashing back to World War 11, and my unit provided extras for the combat scenes. The second movie was *Away All Boats* staring Jeff Chandler and George Nader. In that movie, a naval ship sees action and has to land troops on enemy beachheads at Okinawa. We were the soldiers climbing down the nets to the waiting boats in the water. I had fun, but making a movie required four days of hard work with long hours. Additionally, the director wanted the movie to look realistic—which meant we really had to go full out in our scenes.

I had requested overseas duty during that time and after about a year I was shipped to the Philippines, where I was stationed one year before being transferred to Pearl Harbor, Hawaii. In 1957 Hawaii was not yet a state, so I was still considered as stationed overseas. I served as an MP, and in addition to other training, held flag and Honor Guard duties, and was a member of the Marine Silent Drill Team, performing for President Dwight Eisenhower on Memorial Day.

After a year, I was sent back to California and Camp Pendleton. I was transferred to the Motor Pool 3rd Marine Division. The Motor Pool maintained vehicle and equipment readiness, and in response to a need for vehicles in Japan, my Motor Pool unit was shipped to Japan for 6 months of supplying vehicles for 2 weeks training in war games with South Korea and Japan. Prior to being shipped overseas for that assignment, I enjoyed a thirty-day leave in Dallas. Once I returned to the States, I was discharged.

It was 1959, and I had spent four years and 75 days of service with the United States Marine Corps. I had an opportunity to travel and see parts of the world I had only heard about. It was good experience, and one of which I am proud. In addition to valuable training, I developed a personal discipline and a sense of self that proved to serve me well then, and for many long years after.

The Good Life

Chapter 2

There are always events in any person's life looked back upon as defining moments. Moments that can change you forever. For Glenda, and me there is a "before the assassination" life and an "after the assassination" life; but it has always been a good life.

While home on that 30-day leave before being sent to Japan, I wanted to have some fun and was looking for a date. My brother Bill was taking his girlfriend Jean to a concert, and wanted to know if I was interested in a double date. Johnny Horton, a country and western singer was having a show locally and Jean knew a girl named Glenda who was a fan of Horton's, if I was interested. I was and agreed to meet Glenda on a blind date. I was really attracted to her; she was just a real nice girl and I enjoyed my time with her very much. When I shipped out however, we lost touch. In fact, we had more or less forgotten about each other until a year later, when I got out of the service.

Once discharged and back home in Dallas, I soon managed to get a job at the Ambulance Service Company where my brother was working. The Ambulance Service Company had the contract at that time for the City of Dallas and we responded to all the Dallas emergency ambulance calls. I really loved my job there; it could be challenging at times, but I liked the work. It was definitely a step in the right direction in terms of my boyhood dreams of working in a service related occupation. I was happily employed in emergency services, doing something that was of a service to others, and being paid for it, too.

Of course, I always remembered having met Glenda that time on leave from the Marines. She had definitely made a lasting impression on me, so once I was home again I telephoned her and asked her out. We had our second date in mid March 1960, and by June, Glenda and I had become engaged. Guess you could say we were just meant to be together. Glenda and I were married on August 27, 1960. We had a small church wedding, with a beautiful ceremony celebrated with a few friends and family in attendance. Glenda was thirty minutes late for the ceremony, setting the pattern for much of our married life.

Glenda is an absolutely amazing woman, a wonderful wife and mother; I do not know what I would do without her or what I would be without her. She has always made our home a place I wanted to be, and has faithfully loved and cared for me. The love of my life, she has stood with me through everything life has thrown our way, and I cannot imagine my life without her.

Other than the day I married Glenda, the only other equally thrilling day of my personal life was five years after our wedding, when our son Larry was born on July 10, 1965. Larry has always brought joy to Glenda and me. As a youngster, he was the child every parent longs for: intelligent, athletic, well mannered and never a problem. As an adult, Larry is that and more; he is always selfless and loving, and lives a family centered life. He is also community minded and involved with youth sports at various levels. Larry is a cherished source of pride for Glenda and me. It is easy to say my family is my life; they are my world and I love them.

The first home that Glenda and I had as a newlywed married couple was on Nursery Road in Irving, Texas. Irving had a population of about 45,000 and is located northwest of Dallas city limits and near Dallas-Fort Worth International

Airport is now located. We lived there for about a year before moving into the Oak Cliff area south of the downtown core of Dallas and across the Trinity River.

One of the main reasons we moved from Irving was that the bus system was not good in that area. This was particularly hard for Glenda because at that time in her life she did not have a driver's license. In fact, she did not know how to drive and I was reluctant to teach her because I knew that I just did not have the patience for that. Therefore, we ended up moving back to Dallas where she could get a job and ride the bus to work, it was just a whole lot easier and much more convenient.

The move back to Dallas worked out well for us and we moved back into a one-bedroom efficiency apartment at 222 East Fifth Street in the Oak Cliff section of Dallas. It was a five-unit, single story garden apartment complex somewhat resembling an intimate hotel. It proved to be a very good fit for us at the time, we were comfortable there and it was in a nice area. The complex was directly across the street from a beautiful park called Lake Cliff. The park was nicely maintained with a large lake and vast areas of lawns and greenery. We were also within a short walking distance of Methodist Hospital that is located on Colorado Boulevard and only about five minutes by car from downtown Dallas.

We would actually end up living at that efficiency apartment at 222 East Fifth Street twice. We lived there until mid 1963, at which time we moved into another Oak Cliff apartment located at the corner of Stemmons Avenue and Colorado Boulevard. It was about a half-mile or so to the west from the place on East Fifth Street and almost on the doorstep of Methodist Hospital. The apartment at Stemmons Avenue and Colorado was where we were living at the time of the assassination of President Kennedy.

Living in those days, at least for us, was very laid back and of course, the economy was quite a bit different from what we have today. Mind you salaries were not much compared to today's, but Glenda and I made out okay, we were happy. Glenda's job paid about thirty dollars per week, and mine about forty to forty-five dollars a week. Rent on the apartment was about forty or fifty dollars per month, although we did also have to pay the gas, lights and a water bill, other than the car payments those were all the expenses that we had, so we did very well.

Glenda would usually go to the grocery store with a friend to shop and she would bring home three or four bags of groceries. Stores did not have plastic grocery bags in those days; they used large sized brown paper sacks. Anyway, usually there would be enough groceries for two weeks since I worked every other night and Glenda would just snack when I was working. Food was very inexpensive compared to today's prices. You could get one inch thick T-Bone steaks at meat markets for from twenty-three cents a pound up to thirty-five cents a pound, depending on what store frequented. The price of ground meat ran about nineteen cents a pound and pork chops were about nineteen cents a pound. Back then, shopping in the meat department was a pretty good deal. As I recall, milk came in cartons and they only had half gallons and quarts. We would get milk paying something like fifteen cents a quart. Bread was ten cents a loaf. Vegetables and fruit were cheap in those days too.

My car at that time was a 1957 Ford. The Ford had a standard shift transmission; it was a "three in the tree," slang when I was a young man for a column shift, and had a V-8 engine. It was a lot of fun driving that thing. It was just as fast as it could be and I could really get that car to move.

I loved to drive fast, but Glenda was not quite the fan of speed that I was. Several times, my brother Billy and I went to the local drag strip where I would race small sport cars around a track. On two occasions, I had to tell her what I had done, since I came home with the winning trophy.

Glenda says I was a daredevil, perhaps I was. I loved excitement, and that led me to becoming a rodeo clown. I contacted the local rodeo manager and asked if I could train with him as a rodeo clown, soon I was wearing the big pants, and makeup with a red bulbous nose, chasing bulls when they were not chasing me. A few times I was catapulted though the air because the bull was a little faster than I was in the thick sand of the arena. We would ask friends to join us for the weekend fun, and we often traveled out of town so I could get my kicks in the sandy pens.

About two years into my clown days, I was stomped and mauled very badly by a big bull. Glenda was in the stands with my Dad when it happened. I spent a week in the hospital and only worked one more rodeo as a clown after that narrow brush with death.

Glenda and I really enjoyed the early years of our marriage. If I was off on a Friday or Saturday night, we'd go to the drive-in movies where you could see a double feature for a dollar per car, so sometimes a whole carload of friends would tag along. We would eat hot dogs and popcorn, listening to the voices from the big screen piped into our car from the speaker hanging from the car window. Of course, the films we selected were always action packed.

We shared a nice home in a great area, had friends to socialize with and both held good paying and satisfying jobs. I would say we were happy, in love, lived quite well and had a pretty good time. Our life was good.

Peg O'Neal

Chapter 3

We would be out there on the streets of Dallas taking the shortest, most direct routes at the fastest rate possible, announcing our approach with lights flashing and the siren blaring. In many ways, driving that ambulance was kind of like being a NASCAR driver; we were daredevils racing wildly on city streets, however, our speeding was totally legal.

I worked for the Ambulance Service Company until some time in 1961 when that firm lost the City of Dallas ambulance contract to another area funeral home called Dudley M. Hughes Funeral Home. The Hughes Funeral Home was located on Jefferson Street in Oak Cliff, where the Hughes family lived upstairs. Mr. Hughes was what one expected in a Funeral Director—a smooth voice and manner to match. Once he got the city contract and began to be operational, Mr. Hughes in turn sub-contracted their excess ambulance trade to the O'Neal Funeral Home as well as to a number of other funeral homes around the Dallas area. Thus, the Dudley M. Hughes Funeral Home became the central ambulance dispatching point for southern Dallas. This arrangement provided a much-improved emergency response service for the city of Dallas.

From the 1960s until mid to late 1970s, emergency ambulance service was most often a service provided by local funeral homes. The funeral homes would contract for the city ambulance trade and the funeral homes in turn would get first chance for business on a death when there was one.

That is presumably one of the main reasons that the funeral homes provided the service—for the residual calls or business. Additionally, a firm's name being visible on the side of a vehicle as it sped around town, and on ambulance gurneys at the hospital, was good advertising. The funeral home contract with the city only paid one dollar per call, but the advantage of obtaining business for your mortuary apparently made it worthwhile.

I went to work for Vernon B. O'Neal at the O'Neal Funeral Home & Ambulance Service when I left the Ambulance Service Company. Mr. O'Neal was the owner of the O'Neal Funeral Home and Ambulance Service Company, or O'Neal, Inc. as he usually put at the bottom of the obituary notices that his company placed in the papers.

Mr. O'Neal was affectionately known as Peg to his friends. He gained the nickname as a child when he broke his left leg by getting it stuck in the spokes of his bicycle. His leg failed to heal properly and as a result, it bowed out at the knee. He hobbled along as he walked bowlegged across the floor, much like someone with a wooden leg; so Peg, short for peg leg I guess, became his moniker. Peg O'Neal was a good boss, we knew what he expected, and if we acted in accordance with his policies, he treated us very well.

I loved spending time with Mr. O'Neal in his office, often chatting about life and my wild escapades. He was a chain smoker, somehow oblivious to the fact that the Kool menthol cigarette eternally hanging off one corner of this mouth was bobbing up and down, dropping ashes on his suit as he talked.

One day while passing the time on a slow call day, I started discussing the young spider monkey I had just bought. He wanted to see it in the worst way and told me to run home and it pick up. I brought the monkey to the funeral home in a cage, but Mr. O'Neal wanted to take him out. I tried to warn him it was not a good idea, but he foolishly ignored my caution and put the now free monkey on his desk for a closer look.

The monkey suddenly went wild, running around the big desk sending papers flying into the air like large snow flakes before it leapt to the drapes in his office. A small screeching monkey jumping around the office of a funeral home sounds bad enough, but it is even worse when you learn the monkey was depositing feces at every juncture. Mr. O'Neal wanted me to clean it up, but I told him it was his idea, therefore it was his problem. I scooped up the monkey for the trip home and he called his handyman to clean up the mess.

Mr. O'Neal was also supportive of my weekend job as a rodeo clown, and one day asked me to get into my clown suit so he could see what I looked like. I ran home and got it, returning in full rodeo clown glory. Unexpectedly, an emergency call came in and I had to respond in my clown suit. I must have looked like a nut walking around the hospital in that outrageous outfit, but Mr. O'Neal just laughed it off. He was more than my boss, he was my friend, and when that bull stomped me and I spent that week in the hospital, he generously continued to pay me until I could get back to work.

Peg O'Neal was a character all right, but also a good businessman; he definitely knew how to work a room. He'd hobble around, shaking hands with everyone and introducing himself while making pleasantries. His handshake left something to be desired however, he would offer a limp wrist, grasp the fingertips of the person he was greeting and then more or less wiggle their hand around as if it was a struggling fish.

There were two ambulances at O'Neal's, and each one had two persons assigned to respond to emergencies. The lead driver was the person in charge, normally more experienced, and the person with the responsibility of making the decisions. I left the Marines with the attitude I could handle any job, I was a very confident and energetic person, and well suited for this kind of duty. Since I had some prior experience, it was no surprise to me that Mr. O'Neal assigned me to be his lead driver on ambulance number 606.

Like most ambulances at that time, the ones at O'Neal Funeral Home were actually specially retrofitted and equipped station wagons. We got brand new ones in the fall of 1961. They were 1962 Ford Galaxies as I recall, and they were all fully equipped and stocked for responding to emergency situations. The ambulance had a bench seat in the front and a patient's service area in the rear compartment that was large enough to accommodate at least one full sized emergency ambulance gurney and an attendant's collapsible jump seat.

The rear partition had a linoleum floor for loading and unloading the emergency gurney, with attachments designed to prevent the gurney from moving around within the compartment. This type flooring made sliding the gurney into place relatively straightforward and permitted easy cleaning after transporting an automobile accident patient or other traumatic injury victim. The patient compartment was well supplied with a well-stocked first aid kit, splints, an oxygen tank and mask, and of course, the portable folding ambulance cot or gurney.

For emergency response, the ambulance I drove sported a large red rotating beacon in the center of the roof; positioned closer to the front of the car was a large siren, flanked on each side by two red flashing emergency lights. The name O'Neal was printed on the rear and front side doors of the ambulance, and the unit number 606, a number taken from the vehicle license plate, was displayed on the front windshield near the rear view mirror. The transmission was a three-speed with gear selectors on the steering column, a 289 CID V-8 high performance engine, and extra heavy-duty brakes. It was an extremely fast car and I have to admit it was fun to drive.

The ability to speed was a nice perk in driving an ambulance for the O'Neal Funeral Home, at least to my heavy foot. The Ambulance Service Company where I had worked previously imposed a speed limit on drivers; we could not go any faster than 50 miles per hour, even when responding to a true emergency—even on the freeways. This was a real nuisance, because freeway posted speeds were more than 50 miles per hour. Once we were up to the Ambulance Service Company imposed speed limit on any of the freeways, we might as well have just shut off our siren and lights because we were not going to be passing anything else on the road. In fact, to our chagrin everything else was moving faster than we were. With Mr. O'Neal's ambulance service, it was a completely different story. You pretty much just drove as fast as you felt you needed to, or as fast as you wanted to; and that was right up my alley.

My daily work routine usually started at 8:00 a.m. The commute to work from our place on East Fifth Street in Oak Cliff to the O'Neal Funeral Home located at 3206 Oak Lawn Avenue usually took me about 15 minutes. The funeral home building was on the south side of Oak Lawn and located near the corner of Oak Lawn Avenue and Cedar Springs Road. It is still kind of interesting to drive by the old location where O'Neal's once stood; although the building that had housed O'Neal's is now gone, you can still see the paved driveway we used when going to and from our various emergency ambulance calls.

My primary duty at O'Neal's was to respond to emergency calls. If we weren't out on emergency calls, our daily duties included cleaning the ambulances, inspecting all of the emergency equipment to insure it was working properly, and checking the first aid kits and supplies to make certain that they were well stocked. We never took for granted that another shift had done this, we were committed to providing our patients with the best care we could offer.

In addition to doing odd jobs for Mr. O'Neal, the handyman, Charles washed the ambulances every morning, and Peanuts, my partner and I would dry them. We would use real linens from the service, as pillowcases and sheets had not been replaced by the paper-fabricated ones emergency responders use now.

We worked hard at keeping the vehicles looking their best, partly because we had pride in the vehicle we were driving, and partly because Mr. O'Neal was quite particular about his fleet. He made sure that all of the vehicles were kept clean at all times. He'd even pick over streaks in the window glass that were in some way missed and bits of lint that were deposited on the windows from the sheets that we had used to wipe them off. Of course, there were times when we were busy running calls or when it was raining, that made it occasionally hard to keep the ambulance clean, but we did our best.

Once the vehicles had been washed and serviced, we would address the building interior. We would tidy up the front area, which included the main service entryway and grounds as well as the interior public areas, to ensure that everything was nice and presentable for the clients inside the funeral home. Mr. O'Neal had converted an old house into the funeral home, a common practice back in the '30s and '40s, so it was not like a more modern funeral home building you would see today.

We would then clean up our dormitory, which was supposed to have been done by the shift that was going off, but that would never have happened. It seems that it was always left to Peanuts and me to take care of getting everything in order. The dormitory was an interior room with no windows, and with the door closed and the light off, it was pitch dark in there. Because we worked 24-hour shifts, and the work was so stressful, there were two sets of bunk beds available so you could just lie down and rest or sleep anytime you needed to during the day. We slept when we could.

The dispatcher was in the radio room that was immediately next to the dormitory so he would notify us when an ambulance call came in and we were asleep. We had a company radio and a police radio in our ambulances. When we received a call from the police department, it would come in on our red phone line in the dispatcher's office, which was a direct line phone. They would tell the dispatcher the nature of the call, such as a heart attack or car accident. They would then ask our dispatcher which ambulance was being sent to the call, and the dispatcher would tell them the number of the responding vehicle and then notify the corresponding driver.

Once in the ambulance, we would always check in with the Dallas Police Department dispatcher on the police radio in the car to let them know we were responding. We advised the police dispatcher when we arrived at the location, when we began transporting a patient, and when we arrived at the hospital. I know they needed those times for reports, but I also believe that they kept these times on us because they wanted to make sure that they, and we, were running the city's emergency ambulance service properly and in accordance to their regulations and expectations.

As an ambulance service, we did a lot of business, sometimes responding to as many as twenty calls in a day. Normally, we answered nine or ten calls per ambulance on an average day. Although we answered some serious calls and I had a lot of responsibility, I still had plenty of fun on those ambulances. They were extremely fast vehicles and I loved driving at high-speeds. I wanted to get the patient to medical assistance as soon as possible of course, but mostly I drove fast because it was just plain fun.

I drove the streets of Dallas taking the shortest, most direct route at the fastest rate possible, announcing my approach with lights flashing and siren screaming. People would all be moving or would have already moved off the main roadway, opening a clear path for the ambulance to get to the waiting patient or victim. Driving up on the curb, cutting corners over the sidewalk, squeaking through openings that would scare most people—I loved it all. In many ways, driving that ambulance was rather like being a NASCAR driver; I was a daredevil racing wildly on Dallas city streets, however, my speeding was blissfully legal.

When we were at the funeral home, we would usually be upstairs over the funeral parlors, with the dispatcher or in the dormitory. When we had funeral services downstairs we would take extra caution to be quiet. It was an older building but it was solid, evidently well insulated and sound and noise did not seem to travel through the place all that well. Nevertheless, we were mindfully considerate of the solemnity of the occasion.

We did not participate with funerals as Mr. O'Neal had a staff of funeral attendants who drove the hearse and family cars. On occasion, I would assist with church funeral services, but my main responsibility was running that ambulance as they wanted it done in the city of Dallas.

Peanuts

Chapter 4

I was self-assured when working the ambulance with Peanuts, and maybe overly so. I had served in the military, been overseas, and was confidently determined I had seen just about everything between that and working on an ambulance. Nothing on the job could surprise me; I had seen it all. Until that day in Trauma Room 1, I never imagined just how wrong I could be.

I had quite the reputation at O'Neal's; if you wanted an adrenalin rush, just ride with me. I'd drive on the curb, make harrowing turns—whatever it took to get to the call and transport patients as fast as possible. I also had a pretty good sense of humor; I'd find humor in just about anything as evidenced by my quick wit and occasionally by my wisecracks. I was definitely an extrovert, a real character. Yet, more importantly, I had the reputation as a driver who got things done.

One day when we were changing shifts, Dennis McGuire, the assistant from the other crew confided in me he was quitting unless he could transfer to my shift. He said he and his partner did not really get along well and additionally, he felt his education on the ambulance was lacking because the lead driver did not want to train him. That day they had responded to a nasty car accident with two seriously injured patients. Dennis had not been able to locate some equipment and it had resulted in a argument with his driver. If he could not change drivers, he was quitting. I knew Dennis to be a good man; he was married, had a child and serious about his job.

I explained the situation to my regular assistant, and then to Mr. O'Neal. Dennis became my regular ambulance assistant and I immediately nicknamed him Peanuts. At 5'7," Peanuts was a good five inches shorter than I was, but man was he strong, and a good assistant, too. Over time, he undeniably developed excellent technical skills that were much needed in providing emergency aid on calls. While responding to calls, because the siren was deafening, Peanuts would have to keep the radio receiver to his ear listening for possible additional instructions from the dispatcher, and occasionally balance a map in his lap, ready to provide directions if required. Although we worked together for some time, he had only been my partner for about 3 months when the President was killed.

After completing our daily duties at the funeral building, Peanuts and I would go out for our morning breakfast. At least that is what we would have liked to do; actually, we hardly ever ate breakfast because usually we would be getting calls right off the bat and we would have to head out on those. On most days, we would go to the doughnut shop, grab a couple of doughnuts and a carton of chocolate milk and that would be our breakfast. However, every once in a while, we would get a regular breakfast—eggs and ham, a side of french fries or hash browns and biscuits, but that wasn't very often. Eating a real breakfast was the exception and most often, we just ate a quick bite from the doughnut shop.

We would sometimes try to get breakfast while returning from an early call, picking it up and going back to the funeral home dormitory to eat there. Sometimes we would get a call while we were still eating, then we would head out in the ambulance and try to eat our breakfast on the way, balancing it on our knees as we sped out on the call. Yes, those were some good old days. Peanuts and I had a lot of great fun while being paid to serve our community.

We shared some harrowing times and some hilarious ones as well. I remember one particular call when we transporting to Parkland Memorial Hospital patient familiar to us as problematic. Peanuts was in the back of the ambulance trying to attend to the man who was thrashing violently, pulling at the curtains, and in general creating such a disturbance that I notified the police we needed assistance.

I pulled to the side of Harry Hines Boulevard, went around to the back of the ambulance, and angrily jerked open the rear door. I released the safety on the secured gurney and irately jerked it out the back compartment, thinking Peanuts had hold of the other side. However, his grip had slipped and like some slapstick comedy, the gurney holding our strapped down patient begin rolling down the hill. We chased that gurney, with the patient still yelling and kicking, for two blocks before it bounced off the curb and overturned. Thankfully, the man was not hurt, and the police had not yet arrived, so they missed our mad dash to rescue a patient rolling away just a little faster than we could run – saving us from a lot of potential ribbing.

You get to know a man working 24 hours shifts with him. I got along well with Peanuts and we spent a lot of time together, both in emergency situations and in just talking while waiting for a call. We enjoyed ourselves no matter what happened, and as I like to say, we just got along well, the two of us were well paired.

I do not know what became of Peanuts after I left O'Neal's Funeral Home. We lost contact with each other many years ago. I do know he was sent to Vietnam and was severely wounded while there. Unfortunately, some years later, I heard he had passed away. Looking back, I remember Peanuts as a loyal friend, a dedicated husband and father, and a good assistant. We shared a lot while working together, and I liked him very much.

I was self-assured when working the ambulance with Peanuts, and maybe overly so. I had served in the military, been overseas, and was confidently determined I had seen just about everything between that and working on an ambulance. I had handled myself to the satisfaction of my military superiors, my patients and their families, and my boss. Nothing on the job could surprise me; I had seen it all. Until that day in Trauma Room 1, I never imagined just how wrong I could be.

The Twenty-Dollar Man

Chapter 5

He was a strip club owner, with slicked back hair and a pinky ring that flashed as he gestured in time to his smooth talk. Yes, the man who ingratiated himself with the police, and us, was rough—but he also proved to be a man of his word.

One night in October 1961 or 1962, while employed by Mr. O'Neal, there was a big football game scheduled at the stadium in Dallas between Texas and Oklahoma football teams. The Red River Shootout, as it was known then, was a highly attended annual football game between the University of Oklahoma Sooners and the University of Texas Longhorns. Dallas was chosen as a neutral site since it is located approximately halfway between Austin, Texas and Norman, Oklahoma.

It was a big rivalry game and all manner of people were out for fun, anticipating a good time. Cruising around in cars in the downtown area, they were repeatedly circling the streets in and around Main, Commerce and Elm. There were cars driving bumper to bumper and people were hanging out the windows. The blend of whooping and hollering of the drivers while honking their car horns repetitively in pre-celebration excitement created an expectation for accidents in the minds of the police. Signs on the cars and colors of clothing indicated the university the mobile cheerleaders supported.

Swarms of pedestrians were spilling from the sidewalks into the street. Unbelievably, the jovial spirits of the football fans, as evidenced by the drinking and yelling, was not in any way dampened by the freezing weather. It was bitterly cold so the people huddled in small groups, singing and calling out team chants as they drifted along the street. The air was filled with declarations of team superiority sure to be demonstrated in the game. The Red River Shootout had drawn a huge and boisterous crowd into Dallas, and this was not even the night of the game, insuring increased craziness for the next night.

The local law enforcement agencies, Texas Highway Patrol, Dallas Police Department, and the Dallas County Sheriff's Department had set up a law enforcement command post at the parking lot between the Adolphus Hotel and Baker Hotel on Commerce Street. We were standing by near the police command post because drinking pedestrians and bumper-to-bumper traffic have a way of creating business for ambulances. It was incredibly cold, and Peanuts and I were huddled in the ambulance, the ambulance engine idling as we tried to keep ourselves warm.

Jack Ruby was making the rounds with the nearby command post law enforcement personnel. Jack had one of his employees, walking along with him carrying an urn of hot coffee; he was offering it to the law enforcement people who were struggling to keep warm. When he offered us some, I told him that we did not drink coffee.

Shortly afterward, Jack himself brought us some of the small coke bottles they had back then, along with a bottle opener. He asked us if he could sit with us to keep warm and so we invited him into the ambulance with us. He sat in the attendant's jump seat in the rear compartment of the ambulance and we visited for a short while.

He was smartly dressed in a black, two-piece suit, white shirt, fashionable necktie and a black fedora; he was a dapper fellow perched on the small seat behind us. Jack generously invited us to come and visit his Carousel Club any time that we wanted to. He told us that if we did stop in, that we were to ask for him by name and he would let us in free of charge. He was a strip club owner, with slicked back hair and a pinky ring that flashed as he gestured in time to his smooth talk. Yes, the man who ingratiated himself with the police, and us, was rough—but he also proved to be a man of his word.

Sandwiched between a parking garage and a short-order restaurant, the door to the Carousel Club was located across the street from the Hotel Adolphus on Commerce Street, about 9 blocks or so from Dealey Plaza. The actual club was one flight up a narrow stairway that led from the street level entrance. Like many of the string of nightclubs in the area, the Carousel Club street level entry door was flanked with glass-enclosed displays that announced the entertainment inside. Jack Ruby's Carousel Club display has held photographs of scantily clothed dancers, offering a hint of what could be viewed inside on the three stages inside for a cover charge. At the Carousel Club, dancers stripped down to g-strings and pasties, the legal limit in those days.

Peanuts and I took Jack up on his invitation on several occasions, asking for him by name just as he had suggested, and entering the club free of charge. One time when we visited the Carousel Club, he asked two patrons who were seated alongside the runway to leave their chairs to give Peanuts and I front row seats.

However, fun was not the only thing that brought Peanuts and me to the Carousel Club. One evening we got an ambulance call concerning an injured man on a street side near the Carousel Club. He was lying on the ground with blood oozing from his head. Jack Ruby, who was standing near the unconscious man, approached us nonchalantly. He removed $20, which was a lot of money at that time, from a large wad of bills and handed it to us.

He growled, "That guy was touching one of my girls. When he wakes up, tell him not to bother coming into my club again."

We made an ambulance run to the Carousel Club on another occasion when one of Jack Ruby's girls was having an apparent heart attack. The girl was Shari Angel, a dancer

Jack obviously cared for. We drove her to the hospital as an emergency Code 3, meaning with lights and siren, while Jack followed in his own car. He parked at the hospital on the emergency ramp right in front of our ambulance, and once again peeled off another $20 bill as a gift to us. As it turned out, Shari was not having a heart attack at all, but had been merely hyperventilating from an anxiety attack.

From that point on, Peanuts and I called him "the twenty dollar man"; a colorful and bighearted businessman, we had no idea he was possibly connected to the mob.

The President's Wave

Chapter 6

Peanuts and I were just as animated as those standing on the sidewalk were; we were calling out to the President and First Lady, hoping they would look our way. Then, suddenly the President noticed us perched atop the ambulance. He looked directly at us and smiled as if he knew us. Peanuts and I were thrilled; the President had waved specifically to us.

On November 22th 1963, I went to work at my regular time, and keeping with our daily routine, Peanuts and I did all of our regular chores: cleaned the ambulance, did the required equipment, fuel and building checks, and generally made ourselves ready for whatever the day might bring our way.

Some people may find this hard to believe, but for whatever reason I was quite unaware that President Kennedy was going to be in Dallas that day. I knew the President had planned a trip to Dallas, but I just didn't realize this was the day. I found out about the President's visit when Peanuts mentioned it to me that morning. We talked about watching him from a location close to the funeral home, if we were not out on a call.

I liked President John Kennedy, and related to what he wanted for our country. Although I seldom paid attention to news broadcasts, I did on occasion manage to catch a television or radio program when President Kennedy would be speaking. He was unquestionably a brilliant and amazingly gifted speaker. His style was distinctive and he could really hold my attention. Since his message had a viewpoint that seemed to be directed at me as an individual, I would hang on his every word.

Peanuts and I got an ambulance call at approximately 9AM that morning to respond to the corner of Ervay and Elm Streets for an unconscious person. When we arrived, I observed a disheveled man that appeared to be destitute and homeless. He was an older gentleman, wearing a tattered, heavy overcoat. He told us that he was from New Orleans, Louisiana.

We tried to convince him to go the hospital, as we were concerned he may be ill, but he declined our well-meant suggestions of seeking medical help. He was conscious when we arrived with no obvious injury, and you cannot force anyone into submitting to medical attention against his or her will. Therefore, when it became apparent we could not offer aid or transport the man; we cleared from the call and returned to the funeral home.

At approximately 10:30 or 11:00AM, we were dispatched to yet another emergency ambulance call. This one was for a reported heart attack victim. We picked the patient up at her home and quickly transferred her to Baylor Hospital. After completing the compulsory paperwork, we cleared from Baylor Hospital at approximately 12:05PM with both the police and our dispatcher.

Peanuts and I were going to try to make it back to the funeral home to watch the President's motorcade come down Cedar Springs Road, just half a block to the west from the funeral home. One advantage we had over most people on the street was that we had a police radio in the ambulance and we were able to monitor the progress and the location of the presidential motorcade as it made its way through the city of Dallas.

By monitoring the traffic, we were able to determine we were not going to be able to return to the funeral home in time to see the motorcade pass in that area. Knowing that the motorcade would be coming down Harwood Street, I decided to pull off onto a side street in the area where we already were. I managed to find a location from which we would be able to see the President near the southeast corner of Harwood Street and Cedar Springs Road. I parked the ambulance right there in the roadway.

We were parked behind the waiting spectators who were standing expectantly along the edge of the road. Peanuts and I got out of the ambulance and climbed up onto the hot roof of the ambulance. We took our position and looked out over the heads of the people in front of us just as the motorcade appeared. It is hard to express what I was feeling as the motorcade came into view. I got an amazingly good look at President and Mrs. Kennedy, as the motorcade could not have been traveling any more than about 10 miles per hour when we saw them. I was very excited to see them in the flesh.

The President's car passed directly in front of us, and I noticed there were flags on the front fenders of the long, navy blue limousine that was escorted by motorcycle police. In the front seat were two serious looking men, and seated in the back of the open convertible was Governor and Mrs. John Connally, and the President and First Lady. Man, my heart was racing with exhilaration! The air around us was alive— almost electrically charged with excitement.

The President and Jacqueline Kennedy looked absolutely wonderful, both glowing with happiness. The President was stately, dressed in a suit, waving and smiling broadly at the crowd as they passed. Mrs. Kennedy was wearing a pretty pink suit with a matching hat, her gloved hand waving to the people pressed along the road. They were beaming radiant smiles, and seemed somehow larger than life. Seeing President and Mrs. Kennedy in person was so much better than looking at their photographs and everyone else there must have felt the same, since the noise from the cheering crowd was deafening as they passed us.

Peanuts and I were just as animated as those standing on the sidewalk were; we were yelling and gesturing wildly. The President was brandishing a wide smile and waving pleasantly at the people standing on the sidewalks, and then he noticed us sitting up on that ambulance. At that moment, time froze for me. The President of the United States was looking directly at me; he was smiling and waving as though he had recognized me as an old friend. Peanuts and I were absolutely ecstatic; the President had waved specifically to us!

Aubrey Lee Rike, 6 years old.
April 9, 1944

Aubrey at 12 years old.

Aubrey's Military Service

Boot Camp, 1955

left, Coleman Island Beach, Korea

bottom left, Pearl Harbor, 1958

bottom right, on duty at Pearl Harbor

Aubrey, Glenda, and son, Larry, 1969. Larry is
four years old in this photo.

Larry, Glenda, and Aubrey, August 1983

Aubrey and Glenda's 25th Wedding Anniversary, 1985

Sergeant Aubrey Rike, Highland Park Police Department 1991

Parkland

Chapter 7

I recognized her immediately, having just seen her only minutes earlier in their motorcade. However, at this point, Mrs. Kennedy was not wearing her matching hat; she was not waving and smiling at us as if she knew us. She was trying to run as fast as she could down the hallway with the man on the gurney, who I suddenly came to understand was the President.

Soon after the President's car passed us, as we were still sitting atop our ambulance basking in our good fortune, we got our third emergency call of the day. Someone was apparently having an epileptic seizure in the 100 Block of North Houston Street near the corner of Elm Street. The call was dispatched as such because that was the term the reporting caller used described the event. Peanuts and I proceeded to this next call Code 3, with lights and siren running.

When we got to the location, we found a man lying on the sidewalk on the west side of Houston Street, directly across from the County Jail and Criminal Courts Building Sally-Port entrance. The Sally-Port entrance is where prisoner transfer vehicles would pull in and park to move prisoners in or out of the County Court House and County Jail buildings. Essentially, you entered the space and closed the first door before opening the second to proceed, rather like an airlock.

At the time, the man did not appear to me to have suffered an epileptic seizure. Usually I would have observed drooling, weakness or lack of coordination, and scuffed shoes or extremities as a result of thrashing on the ground. The only symptoms I observed were a small abrasion on the middle of his forehead and faintly incoherent speech when I questioned him. Subsequently, in view of the fact that he could have had a head injury that prevented him from providing needed pertinent information, we drove him to Parkland Memorial Hospital responding Code 3.

My reasoning for transporting him was that he did have physical evidence of a head injury and exhibited obvious mental confusion; therefore, regardless of the source of his head injury he needed medical attention. With head injuries, the prudent thing to do is get the patient to a hospital to be examined more thoroughly as soon as possible. The other thing I considered was that there was already a fairly large crowd gathered, and the President's motorcade was due to pass that exact location within another 10 minutes or so. If we were going to move him, it needed to be soon.

While we were transporting our patient to Parkland Hospital, the presidential convoy had continued its way south on Harwood Street, then to Main Street and into Dealey Plaza. As the motorcade made its way through the plaza manipulating the zigzag Main-Houston-Elm Street turns, the President would be shot just a few hundred feet from where we had been standing just minutes before.

I took a different route to Parkland Memorial Hospital than the one the driver of the President's limousine would take. I drove west on Elm Street and went underneath Stemmons Freeway. I then went north on Industrial Boulevard, past the Trade Mart where President Kennedy was scheduled to speak, and eventually turned left onto Harry Hines Boulevard and Parkland Memorial Hospital.

A very large facility, even by the standards of that time, Parkland Memorial Hospital was well equipped, and as a major trauma center it boasted an emergency room staff very familiar with serious injuries. Additionally, Parkland Memorial was a Dallas County publicly funded hospital. As a result, between accepting indigent patients and being a first choice for serious injuries, Parkland Memorial was a very busy hospital.

Meanwhile, a frantic call had been placed from the Dallas Police radio room to the emergency desk at Parkland Memorial. The details were limited; there had been a shooting involving the President and his party and they were on their way to Parkland Memorial. A whirlwind of activity began behind the scenes as hospital officials hurriedly started to move some of the patients with lesser injuries away and out of the emergency department.

However, this activity was yet unknown to Peanuts and me, and the excitement of seeing the President had dimmed with the normal routine of work. At about 12:35 PM we stood just inside the front entryway of the emergency department with our head injury patient, waiting to get him registered at the emergency desk prior to examination. We had unloaded our patient from the ambulance, but still had him on our gurney.

Suddenly, men dressed in suits came running into the emergency room. However, it was not their alarmed faces that shocked me; I was stunned to see they were brandishing shotguns and green colored machine guns. Suddenly, the normal routine of our day had erupted into terrifying pandemonium.

The men, who we later identified as Secret Service agents, were screaming, hollering, and cursing while insistently demanding for someone to get them gurneys. One of the men rapidly approached us, adamantly shouting that we get our patient off our gurney, because he wanted it.

My impudent response was "Hey, I'm not looking to release this man, because he hasn't paid yet." Taken off guard, what I said was probably a bit nastier than that, but that is close enough. Our normal routine required us to obtain enough information on our patient to permit O'Neal's to invoice the person for the services that we had provided, and I was determined to do just that.

I did not know at the time the frantic man was a US Secret Service Agent, as he never presented credentials or a badge, and we still had not heard that the President had been shot. At about this same time I happened to see Vice President Lyndon Johnson come staggering into the emergency area. He was unassisted and alone, just leaning on the wall for support. Bypassing everyone in the room, he walked right into Minor Medicine, which was directly across from the Registration Desk where Peanuts and I were standing with our patient.

Vice President Johnson looked to me to be quite pale and I looked over at Peanuts and said quietly under my breath, "I guess the old SOBs done had another heart attack and that's what this is all about."

By that time, the unruly group of men had managed to get a couple of empty hospital gurneys out to the ambulance dock. I watched in dismay as they brought in the Governor of Texas, John Connally. I was astonished to see he was bleeding very badly; blood was dripping, or more like pouring, off of the gurney and from his right arm onto the hospital corridor's tiled floor. The small group of people who entered with the injured Governor began running down the hallway from the emergency room lobby to an area designated Emergency Major Medicine, located approximately fifty feet from the emergency desk where we were standing.

A short ten seconds later, my attention was focused again on the emergency room doorway as even more men brought in another gurney and began to push it frantically past us towards Emergency Major Medicine. A man wearing a suit was lying on his back with his knees bent, his legs in a propped up position. The man's head was covered with a suit coat.

Then I saw the pink suit. Jacqueline Kennedy was holding onto the gurney as they ran down the hall towards Emergency

Major Medicine. I recognized her immediately, having just seen her only minutes earlier in their motorcade. However, at this point, Mrs. Kennedy was not wearing her matching hat; she was not waving and smiling as if she knew us. She was hanging onto the gurney and trying to run as fast as she could down the hallway with the man on the gurney, who I suddenly came to understand was John Kennedy, President of the United States.

The nurse at the emergency admissions desk broke this surreal scene by telling us to take our patient back to Emergency Major Medicine for treatment. We took the patient back and placed him in one of the treatment cubicles in the emergency room there in Major Medicine. I assisted him in moving from our ambulance gurney and onto the hospital gurney where he could wait to be seen by a doctor. It was cubicle number eight, which was located immediately next to the doors of the X-Ray Room.

Chapter 8

This brief case was attached to his left wrist with a set of handcuffs. I believe it was the legendary "football" which accompanied President Kennedy on every move that he had ever made and that he might possibly continue to make...as President of the United States.

The Secret Service agents must have been paying close attention to what Peanuts and I were doing and where we were in the hospital. Once we had our gurney empty, the same Secret Service agents that had approached us out front minutes earlier, told us we were going to be transferring the President to St. Paul Hospital, located just a few blocks from Parkland Memorial Hospital. I suspect the reason they wanted us to take the President to St. Paul Hospital is that it was a Catholic hospital and the President was Catholic. A Secret Service agent and a motorcycle officer escorted Peanuts and I out to the ambulance dock to have us put the clean sheets on the ambulance gurney. Prior to going out to the ambulance, they warned us that we had better not talk to anyone or say anything about what was going on inside the hospital. They stressed in no uncertain terms, if we failed to heed their warning they would "knock our friggin' heads off." Only it was not friggin'—it was much more severe than that.

As we left the building, we noticed that the President's limousine was parked in the stall immediately to the left of our ambulance. We had backed our vehicle into the stall so the rear doors were adjacent to the hospital emergency room doors to unload our patient, but the President's limousine had been pulled headfirst into the ambulance bay. We could see people with buckets and sheets trying to clean blood from the limousine. I could also see the roses that Mrs. Kennedy had received earlier that day at Love Field, laying on the bloody back seat.

While we were redressing the gurney, President Kennedy had been placed in Trauma Room 1 and emergency medical procedures were being feverishly administered. Doctor Phillip Earl Williams found a folding metal chair that he brought to the trauma room corridor and placed to the left of the doorway of Trauma Room 1, so that the First Lady had something to sit on while she waited for word on her husband's condition.

Peanuts and I finished putting the clean sheets on our ambulance gurney and we hurried back to Emergency Major Medicine. The Secret Service by this time had made it abundantly clear they were in charge of directing our movements, including where to sit. They indicated for us to take a seat on a hospital gurney that was positioned along the left hand wall of the trauma corridor immediately outside of the now empty Trauma Room 2. As I understood it, they had already taken Governor Connally from that room up to surgery. We were directed to wait on a gurney placed against the wall directly across from Trauma Room 1 where President Kennedy was being treated. Unbelievably, Jacqueline Kennedy was sitting in a folding metal chair directly across the hallway from us.

There were several people, doctors and nurses, going in and out of Trauma Room 1 to provide medical care and different supplies for various procedures. Peanuts and I never moved; we just sat across from Mrs. Kennedy in that hallway as we had been instructed to do by the Secret Service agents. The hallway was no more than eight feet across and so we were literally only about five feet away from her. It was an amazing situation to experience.

There seemed to me to be a whole lot of confusion inside of the large lobby area of Emergency Major Medicine. Located just to our right, many of the dignitaries and other significant people of the day had gathered there. It was a sizable crowd and they were quite noisy. In the midst of the confusion, I could not help but notice that there was a high-ranking military aide, a two star general I believe, standing about eight to ten feet off to our immediate right. He was standing quite close to Trauma Room 1 where President Kennedy was undergoing emergency medical care.

I do not know exactly when he had arrived or stationed himself there; I just recall suddenly noticing him. He was not there when Peanuts and I were first escorted to the hospital gurney in the hall outside the trauma rooms. But somehow, amid all the confused, yelling and scurrying men, a two star general had appeared; and he had a medium sized, almost square shaped, hard shell, black leather briefcase in his left hand. Amazingly, the briefcase was attached to his left wrist with a set of handcuffs. I believe it was the legendary "football" which accompanied President Kennedy on every move that he had ever made and that he might possibly continue to make as President of the United States. It contained the coding mechanism that would be necessary to launch nuclear weapons in the event of a required emergency nuclear strike or retaliation.

The general with the briefcase handcuffed to his wrist stood motionless, apparently indifferent to the milling mob just beyond Trauma Room 1. He was not with Lyndon Johnson in Minor Medicine, a fact I hoped to be the best possible visible indication that the patient in that room was of vast global significance, and that he was as yet, the living Commander In Chief of the United States Armed Forces.

There was a growing group of people, probably fifty or sixty, who were inside the emergency room lobby area of

Emergency Major Medicine. Of course, there were no radio or television reporters or photographers, because Secret Service agents were tenaciously guarding the entry door of Emergency Major Medicine and would not let anybody in or out who was not supposed to be there. The group was comprised for the most part of law enforcement officials, employees of government agencies and local and state dignitaries. However, they were not behaving like public servants or public figures.

There were loud accusations going back and forth between members of the FBI, the Secret Service and others. There was a lot of talk about a communist conspiracy and the possibility of someone trying to overthrow the government of the United States. Voices raised by flaring tempers were becoming increasingly more frequent. Some of the men and most of the women were crying openly while others stood frozen in place, apparently in shock. Some were making shrill, heated accusations insisting that various agencies in charge that day had failed to do their jobs properly. Others raced from one place to the other, trying to organize the proceedings or perhaps responding to the incessant demands of their superiors.

At various times I saw several men reach inside their jackets menacingly, apparently threatening to pull out a concealed handgun while in intense arguments. I feared things could easily get out of hand without much provocation. Obviously, the situation was growing dangerously unstable. Men were jostling and jockeying for position while trying to assume control, raised voices all over the room were growing evidence of escalating disagreements; it was a type of chaos I had never seen. In direct conflict with what their normal jobs may have been, I felt anything but safe with so many armed men in such close proximity.

I think about the people who were there: Secret Service Agents, FBI Agents, Dallas County Deputies, Dallas Police Officers, Texas State Police Officers, the Mayor and his wife, Texas State Attorney General Waggoner Carr, Congressmen,

Senators, and other special guests assembled to meet the President and Mrs. Kennedy. It was all quite astonishing and unimaginable that these people would behave so poorly under the circumstances, and yet there they were, acting just as crazy as could be. All of these supposedly refined people were so busy assigning blame and cursing each other, that the tension of the moment became perversely amusing to Peanuts and me. It was a struggle not to laugh, our nerves were kicking in I guess, but somehow we managed to stifle ourselves and keep a relatively sober face. Especially since, we were face to face with Jacqueline Kennedy.

I felt incredibly sorry for Mrs. Kennedy; she was just sitting there, an exceptionally calm presence in a storm of controversy, unable to escape their foul language and astonishing poor behavior, which was all the more shocking considering who these people were. You would expect that they might have been making some effort to have a little more consideration for her under the circumstances. I mean, good manners in those days dictated that regardless of the circumstances, you just did not curse in front of a lady in Texas; they probably do now, I suppose.

Smoke Break

Chapter 9

The smoke drifted up and away from her hair, away from her sad eyes and the bloody pink suit. She sat on a hard, cold, metal chair — alone in the hallway, waiting for the dreaded outcome of her visit to Dallas. I had done what she asked, but I wish I could have done more.

S itting on the hard gurney in the hallway across from Mrs. Kennedy, I suddenly realized, I needed a smoke, and in those days you could smoke anywhere you wanted to, even inside of a major city hospital emergency area. I was out of cigarettes at the time, so I gestured to a Secret Service agent standing at the trauma corridor entranceway to move toward me.

Once he got to where we were sitting, I asked him quietly if I could go out front and get a package of cigarettes. He said, yes and told another Secret Service agent and a motorcycle police officer to escort me. The cigarette machine was in the waiting room, which was out front in the hospital's emergency department main entrance. The waiting room was for people who were waiting to be seen by a doctor, or people waiting for someone currently being treated to be released.

Of course, many of the people habitually found there were people we called ambulance chasers—people who just hang around Parkland Memorial Hospital all day and often also long into the night, watching the ambulances come in and out. These people would try to get a look at whatever they could in any emergency case, fascinated by blood and always curious as to what had happened. Of course, over time, they all get to know the regular ambulance drivers and the chasers in the waiting room were now hollering and asking questions of me.

One particular fellow furtively whispered, "Al! What is going on back there? How's the President? How bad is he, Al?"

Ignoring him, I remained focused on getting the cigarettes. I was not going to acknowledge the chaser, because the Secret Service had repeatedly told me what they were going to do to me if I did say something. In the unlikely event I might have forgotten their threats, the Secret Service agent and motorcycle police officer were standing right next to me as glaring reminders. I just minded my own business and paid no attention to the chasers calling out questions; I was there to get cigarettes and nothing else.

Once I got the cigarettes, the three of us started walking back down the hallway from the waiting room toward Emergency Major Medicine. Just up ahead of us in the hallway were two Secret Service agents standing outside the door to Emergency Major Medicine checking credentials before allowing anyone access. There was a man in a blue suit briskly walking about twenty-five feet in front of us. He stopped at the door and although we could not hear the conversation, we saw him reach abruptly inside his coat. When he did, the two Secret Service agents grabbed him, put his hands behind his back and forcefully threw him to the floor. When they reached into his jacket and pulled out a gun, I was really frightened. When they next discovered credentials showing that he was an FBI agent, they allowed him to get up, and they brushed him off and let him in. It was like a movie, the good guys looking for the bad guys.

When I got back to the gurney and Peanuts, I told him about the incident that had happened out in the hall with the FBI agent. We both, under our breath of course, were giggling and snickering that an FBI agent had accidently been on the receiving end of such violent treatment. We did not want to be disrespectful to the First Lady, so we quickly got our impulses under control; it would not have been right, you know, us laughing while she was grieving.

I lit up a cigarette and as I was smoking it Mrs. Kennedy looked over at me and quietly asked, "May I have a cigarette?"

A little surprised, I said, "Sure," jumped down off the gurney, and approached her. The cigarettes were still packed very tight in the package and I was trying to pull one out for her when the Secret Service agent who had just allowed me to get the cigarettes grabbed me by the arm. He twisted my arm unsympathetically, as he pulled the package of cigarettes out of my hand. In his overstated efforts toward security, he then pulled the top of the package completely off and cigarettes went flying everywhere.

Once assured it was just an ordinary pack of cigarettes, he growled, "Now, give me a light."

I thought, "*Man, this guy is a real ass.*" Nevertheless, I nervously extended my Zippo to him. He jabbed my lighter back toward me and the now glowing cigarette was handed to Mrs. Kennedy. Suddenly, the FBI agent being thrown to the floor did not seem quite so funny.

Approximately 15 or 20 minutes later a young candy striper came down the hallway in her red and white uniform. Candy Stripers were young women 15 to 16 years old who did volunteer work for the hospital. The candy striper had brought a silver service tray with a nicely arranged coffee service for Mrs. Kennedy. However, when the girl poured the coffee and extended it to Mrs. Kennedy, the Secret Service agent grabbed the girl's arm, and took the coffee cup, sipping from it. He must have decided it was safe, as he immediately put it down and pushed a second cup on the tray towards the girl, indicating she was to pour another cup for Mrs. Kennedy.

Mrs. Kennedy drank the coffee and when finished, I believe the Secret Service agent took the coffee cup from her.

Mrs. Kennedy had been sitting there for some time when she asked, "Are you young men from Dallas?" and of course, we answered, "Yes."

I really do not remember if anything else was said. I have often thought many times long since then, what I would have said, if I had could have managed to say anything? Might I have said, "Yes ma'am, and are you from Washington?" I just do not recall saying anything further. It is difficult for an ordinary person to talk to someone like Mrs. Kennedy. Of course, everyone in America knew and loved her. She was known to be intelligent and cultivated, and had brought to the White House a natural sense of style and elegance. Jacqueline Kennedy had won the heart of a nation, mine included. Nevertheless, she was still the wife of the President of the United States. It would have been hard to make small talk under normal conditions, and was all but impossible under the given circumstances.

She had small bits of tissue, and absorbed bloodstains all over the front of the suit she was wearing. The suit was pink, and looked like a nubby thick terry cloth. She seemed oblivious to us sitting there, focused on the blood on her hands and clothing. Anyway, it seemed she was trying to wipe the blood away with her hands. I went to the scrub room that was immediately adjacent to Trauma Room 2, and got her a wet towel. I brought it out to her and looking up, she softly thanked me. We watched as using the towel, she removed most of the blood leaving just a few stains as silent testament to the horror she was enduring.

When she got through with the towel, she put it discreetly underneath her chair. I did not want her to have to see her husband's blood again, so I walked over to the side of her, bent down and told her I was going to take the towel. She thanked me again and I took the towel, and put it in the bin with the dirty towels in the scrub room. I returned to my place on the gurney in the corridor without speaking, but wishing there was more I could do for her.

Throughout the entire time that Peanuts and I sat there across from Mrs. Kennedy I never saw her go into Trauma Room 1. She sat very still, silently seated on a folding metal chair waiting for official word on the condition of the President. I never saw anyone comfort her or ask what he or she could do to make things more bearable. Although you could see she was distressed, and probably in shock, she was not attended to in any manner. However, I also never saw her cry. She just sat on that hard, cold, metal chair; sat alone in the hallway, waiting for the inevitable dreaded outcome of her visit to Dallas.

The Casket

Chapter 10

My vision was blurred by tears as I watched her kiss his hand and silently say goodbye. Such private moments are never meant to be shared with others. That she was forced to do so was somehow offensive, and increased my heartache for her loss.

As Peanuts and I were still sitting on the hospital gurney in the corridor, a Secret Service agent came up to us and announced the President was dead. He asked us if we worked for a mortuary.

I told him, "We work for a funeral home, yes sir."

In a resigned voice he said, "Well, we're going to need a casket to put the President in to carry him back to Washington."

I said, "Okay." and jumped down from the hospital gurney. I went to the nursing station desk in Emergency Major Medicine where I used their telephone and placed a call to Mr. O'Neal.

When I got Mr. O'Neal on the line, he told me that someone had already notified him of the need for a casket and that he was in the process of getting one ready and loaded for delivery. While placing the call to Mr. O'Neal, I glanced into treatment stall number eight where Peanuts and I had earlier placed our patient. It was empty, our patient had evidently been treated and left, maybe had been told to leave by the FBI, or perhaps the fear I had experienced earlier had resulted in his just walking out of the hospital.

When advising us about the need for a casket, the Secret Service agent had also told us to go into Trauma Room 1 and prepare the President's body. They wanted us to clean his remains and prepare him for placement into the casket.

Trauma Room 1 was about a twelve feet by fourteen feet area, just large enough to allow working room on all sides of a gurney, and yet small enough to easily observe what was present and for quiet conversations to be heard.

When I first got into the trauma room, one of the things I remember seeing almost immediately was the President's discarded clothing; his suit, shirt, tie and other articles of clothing were lying in a corner of the room. The suit jacket had a pin stripe. The shirt was a white dress shirt with a blue striped pattern. The President's body was lying on the emergency treatment table and it was completely covered with a clean, white sheet.

Peanuts and I pulled the sheet back to see what amount of blood and other debris we were going to have to clean up, and also to determine if there would be anything else we might have to do. The President's head was completely covered with a sheet. The sheet had been swathed around his head, several times overlapping over itself; you could not see his head or his face at all. The only people present at that time were Nurse Doris Nelson, Head Nurse of the Emergency Department at Parkland Memorial Hospital and Peanuts and I.

Looking at the President I first noticed that he had a bad slit or a cut on his throat and speaking of the tracheotomy I said to Nurse Nelson, "That's the sloppiest 'trach' I've ever seen."

The unusually jagged incision appeared to me to be a little more than an inch in length, positioned vertically down the center of his throat. Years later, after I had many times described the wound as vertical, I came to realize I was mistaken about the orientation of the wound. Looking back,

I remember the President's head was tilted back, elongating the neck. This must have resulted in the wound gaping open, suggesting to me the incorrect vertical incision instead of the correct left to right, horizontal alignment.

Nelson replied, "Well we did a 'trach' there, but it is also a bullet wound."

The President also had several cut-downs in his arms and ankles. It seemed like an excessive number of cut-downs, more than I had ever seen, and I had seen plenty cut downs in emergency rooms. Peanuts and I turned the President over onto his side with his front toward us so that we could support the body while determining if he had any blood on his back that would need to be removed. We noticed that fluids had already begun to settle into the tissues of his back as a result of gravity, resulting in splotches of black, blue and even purple where the blood had pooled in livor mortis.

I never detected any wounds in the President's back at all, nor did I see one in his shoulder. Of course, we were not looking for wounds in any area; the purpose of our brief examination was to determine what steps were needed to clean the body for placement into the casket. Looking back, of course, hindsight being what it is, it would have been interesting to have a closer look for such a wound, but we did not examine the body, nor were we authorized to do so. There were a few places of dried blood on the skin of the President's back that we did not attempt to remove since they were quite well dried, and so we simply pulled the sheet back over his body and head.

In this particular case we were asked to simply ensure the basic and immediate sanitary needs of the body were addressed, much of which had already been seen to by Nurse Doris Nelson and her staff, and then to place the President in the casket for transportation to Washington. After having had a fairly thorough look at the body to determine what cleaning, if any, we needed to do; we had wrapped or enshrouded the President in a clean white hospital sheet.

At approximately 1:45 PM Mr. O'Neal appeared, signaling the arrival of the casket to be used to transport the President's body. When a casket is pulled from the rollers in the rear compartment of a hearse, it slides onto the top of a church truck, which is a folding mechanical dolly with four wheels that allows the casket to be wheeled around rather than being hand carried. The FBI had someone accompany me outside, where I placed the casket on the church truck and pushed it back to Trauma Room 1.

It was scary out there, a large crowd had gathered and a strong police presence was making itself known. People were yelling at me asking questions, but I tried to keep my head down and concentrated on the job at hand; the FBI had made it very clear they wanted no information leaking from Peanuts and me, and they had also made the consequences of doing so very clear. We could talk, but the results would be a physical beating or possibly worse.

We moved the casket Mr. O'Neal had brought from the funeral home into Trauma Room 1. In preparation of moving the body, we opened the lid and placed the casket along side of the bed or the emergency gurney that the President was laying on so that we could pick him up to transfer him into the casket.

At this moment, Jacqueline Kennedy came walking in with a Secret Service agent and Nurse Nelson. Mrs. Kennedy walked up to the left side of the President, near his waist and stopped. I remained standing at the President's head, Peanuts and Nurse Nelson backed up to make room for her as she approached the body, and stood against the wall behind her, the Secret Service agent had lingered near the door. After a few moments, a solemn Mrs. Kennedy gradually reached out and grasped the sheet, slowly pulling it back to reveal her husband's nude body down to his waist.

His head and face were wrapped in a sheet, but she looked up and down at what was exposed of his body as we stood motionlessly in place. After a few moments, she removed her wedding band and then lifting President Kennedy's left hand tried to place it on his finger. Of course, his ring finger was twice as big as her finger and it was instantly obvious the ring was not going to fit. Undeterred, she kept pushing on the little gold band, as if forcing it were possible.

I could see she needed some assistance, so I retrieved a tube of surgeon's gel from the emergency medical supplies cabinet and applied it to the President's finger. Mrs. Kennedy again attempted to push the ring on, but even with the slickness of the gel, it became apparent it was not going to fit. Mrs. Kennedy must have realized this; she stopped struggling and resigned herself to leaving her wedding band wedged just below the knuckle of her slain husband's finger.

Silently, she bent over and gently kissed the ring on his hand and that simple gesture instantly brought tears to our eyes, it was an indescribably emotionally charged moment. In those few minutes, she was more than the First Lady, and he was more than the President; he was her husband and she was his wife. During those hushed moments, she was a just woman who loved a man who had died, and she was saying goodbye. Jacqueline Kennedy had been forced to share her private grief with strangers. Those types of personal moments are never meant to be shared with others. That she was forced to do so was offensive to me, and swelled my heart with increased anguish for her loss.

Mrs. Kennedy left the room and the somber quiet was broken by a Secret Service agent saying to us, "Okay, let's get him loaded up. Let's go." Peanuts and I moved together towards the President.

To pick up a body two persons stand on the same side of the deceased to be moved. One person supports the head and upper torso by putting one hand underneath the neck to brace the head and keep it from falling back, and then he puts his other hand in the small of the back. Then the assistant puts his hand adjacent to the first person's hand in the small of the patient's back and his other hand underneath the deceased's calves of his legs just below the patient's knees. Then together you roll the deceased towards you so the body is cradled in your arms before you lift it off the gurney.

The first time we began to pick up the President, I put my right hand underneath his head; I could feel the back of the skull had been blown out—it was literally blasted away. I felt the serrated edge of the hole in the skull on my hand. It was not painful, but I could feel the jagged edges of the bones through the sheet on the palm of my hand. I could also feel the President's brain shifting in my hand within the hole located just to the right of the center of the head. Then, as I moved my hand further to put my arm further underneath his neck in order to lift him, I noticed my hand was covered with the President's blood and his blood was also on the cuff and forearm of the right sleeve of my shirt.

I feared the blood would continue to seep from the swaddling around his head into the casket interior, so we replaced the body on the gurney. I wiped my hands clean and I asked Nurse Nelson if she could get us a rubber sheet to put inside the casket. I wanted to roll up the edges to make a dam in the casket interior so the blood would not wick down into the lining and stain it.

It was a solid bronze casket and weighed about 400 pounds when empty. The interior was lined in very expensive white silk. The purchase price of cars in those days was about $2000. In fact, the ambulance we were driving cost $2000 and the casket that O'Neal brought was for a $3000 service, which meant the embalming, use of the chapel for the service, use of the hearse and family car and graveside amenities totaled $3000. Therefore, you can see how expensive that casket was; it cost more than a new car. Anyway, I thought sure they would bury him in that expensive casket and Mr. O'Neal thought the same thing. Consequently, we got the white rubber sheet; I rolled up the edges and made it into a little dam so it would catch the blood that was seeping out of the President's head.

People may wonder about how this made me feel, handling the President's body and dealing with his blood on my sleeve. I cannot speak for Peanuts, but as for myself, I do not know that I necessarily felt any different about doing these things for the President, than I have felt in doing the same thing for someone else. It may sound dispassionate to people who are not in the funeral service or ambulance profession, but you just do what needs to be done. You do all you can, the best way you that know how, and you hope that whatever you do is going to be alright or acceptable and hopefully of assistance or comfort to the grieving family.

Looking back after all these years, I recall that on some level, the experience of handling the President's body was almost like any other call or case. He was essentially just another dead human body, another person now gone that was loved by others, another victim of death needing to be handled, cleansed, and casketed.

In some professions there is a somewhat detached feeling you have to employ that gives you the ability to perform that kind of duty; doctors, nurses, police officers and others that deal with the harsher side of life know this objectivity. This professional indifference was what made it possible for me to get through what were otherwise unquestionably the worst parts of that day. But, I distinctly recall that several times during the day I was anything but detached; in fact, I definitely felt moved emotionally, and in many ways my feelings were similar to those that I experienced with the death of a young child; helpless and searching for a way to make things better.

Last Rites

Chapter 11

Mrs. Kennedy was holding onto the side of the casket and I was at the head trying to move out the door and from the hallway someone with the city or the state or maybe the county snarled, "You're not going anywhere with him!" While the Secret Service agent ordered gruffly, "Get out of the way. We are moving him!" I cringed inwardly, the fight in the other room had moved to us.

A s we began again to try to place the President in the casket, someone in the trauma room mentioned that he had not had the Last Rites administered to him. Therefore, a priest was contacted and summoned to the hospital. Mrs. Kennedy left the room, but we were instructed to remain in Trauma Room 1.

We waited about 30 or 40 minutes, although it seemed like an eternity to me before two priests entered the room, introduced as Father Huber and Father Thompson. Father Huber was compassionately attentive to Mrs. Kennedy. In a soft voice, he spoke briefly with her before beginning his task of administering the Final Sacrament. He then placed a purple colored stole around his own neck before approaching the President's body.

I stood at the head end of the gurney and watched Father Huber as he pulled at the sheet that wrapped the President's head. The sheet had been wound multiple times around the President's head. Pulling at an edge where it overlapped upon itself, the priest pulled a section down revealing a small portion of the forehead, but left the President otherwise completely covered. From my position I could not see the President's forehead, nor did I see a head wound. Father Huber then anointed the President's forehead with oil while praying in Latin. The prayer completed, the priest adjusted the wrapping to cover the President's head once more.

When the priest continued his prayers in English, Mrs. Kennedy's heartbreaking voice was heard in soft response. Father Huber blessed the body and then focused on the interior of the adjacent open casket, sprinkling it with holy water. Suddenly still, he nodded to me, indicating he had finished administering the sacrament. Peanuts and I then lifted the President and placed him in the open casket. We closed the casket lid, sealed it and the priest placed a crucifix on top of the casket. The priest stepped to the doorway, where Mrs. Kennedy thanked them for their prayers and kindness.

It has been reported by various writers and assassination researchers over the years since 1963 that one of the casket handles was damaged during the transfer of President Kennedy from Dallas back to Washington, DC. Many people believe that this damage resulted from passing the casket through the door of Air Force One while the handle was pivoted in the outward carrying position. However, I feel that the casket handle may have been possibility damaged at Parkland during the following struggle.

After casketing the President's body, the Secret Service would not let us out of the trauma room. This seemed just fine with me as being inside of Trauma Room 1 seemed the safest place for us to be, as the arguing and shouting was still going on in Major Medicine among the various authorities who were out there. In fact, the only place I really felt safe was in Trauma Room 1. At about the time that we were preparing to exit the trauma room with the casket, a nurse, possibly Doris

Nelson, entered the room. She was carrying a brown Safeway Grocery paper sack. She picked up the President's clothing from the trauma room floor and placed it the Safeway sack.

Then the Secret Service agent instructed, "Let's go!" and we started out the trauma room door with the casket.

Mrs. Kennedy was standing behind us holding onto the casket, and I was at the head of the casket as we were trying to move out the door where some official looking persons were adamantly insisting, "You're not going anywhere with him!"

The Secret Service agent demanded furiously, "Get out of the way. We *are* moving him!" The brawl in the other room had moved to us.

The Dallas County Coroner was Doctor Earl Rose. He was there in the corridor outside of the trauma room claiming that according to Texas State Law he had to retain the body long enough to perform an autopsy. The federal authorities evidently did not see things that way and they were clearly of a mind that they were going to take the President's body back to Washington immediately, regardless of what anybody had to say to the contrary.

There was no federal statute in the United States yet in 1963 that made the assassination of a U.S. President a federal legal matter. There was a statute in effect in Dallas County in Texas as there was in every county in every state of the union indicating that when there was a death such as a murder or a shooting death, an autopsy was required in the jurisdiction of the county where the crime was committed before the body could legally leave that county.. In any case, once the body was removed without these matters being fulfilled, the chain of custody for evidence could possibly be compromised or lost.

Then the Secret Service agent again ordered, "Let's go!" As much as we preferred the relative safety and the quiet of the trauma room to what was going on in the rest of the Major Medicine area, we started out the door with the casket. Then the struggle really began.

The local authorities pushed us back in and again the Secret Service agent pushed back still angrily demanding, "Let's go!" and again we would vainly attempt to move forward, only to be pushed back once more. We would push the casket forward through the doorway of Trauma Room 1 and into the corridor, and then the local Dallas County people would push it back into the room. This went on for what it seemed to me like ten minutes. We repeated that movement of a few steps forward and then back repeatedly, like an obscene dance.

All the while, Mrs. Kennedy was standing at the back of the casket of the President and the priest was trying to walk alongside the juggled casket. He was blessing the casket with holy water as if oblivious to the ongoing struggle. The crucifix that he had put on the casket was being jerked around so much by the ensuing tug-of-war that despite the strength of the magnetic adaptors on its back, the crucifix was sliding off; I twice grabbed it and centered it back on the casket.

The crucifix that we placed on the casket for the President was a high quality metal crucifix that had some very strong magnets on the back of it to hold it securely onto the casket lid. I had assisted at some Catholic funeral services, and observed many of the Catholic services that O'Neal Funeral Home had performed. I had never seen a crucifix slide or move in any way when attached with the magnet, they always hold pretty strong. We had to stop twice and get that casket put back on the truck to keep it from falling off and onto the floor. The area was like a wild mob scene; people were pushing and shoving, and doing a whole lot of cursing.

I could hear people hollering, "It was *your* mother f***ing fault!"

"That son-of-a-bitch was supposed to be doing this..."

"F*** this!" and "F*** that."

Of course, they used the real "F" word, but that is not the kind of language I could repeat. It was a real nasty environment, and I thought at the time, to just remain in Trauma Room 1 would have been so much nicer and safer.

We finally made our way down the corridor inching forward a few feet at time, until we were about even with Obstetrics & Gynecology. I estimate we had traveled about 30 to 25 feet down the wide corridor toward the doorway, with another 25 feet to traverse.

Abruptly somebody standing back at about Trauma Room 2, called out, "Let the son-of-a-bitch go! Theran Ward has said that he'd sign the death certificate."

Everybody reluctantly backed off, and we quickly moved out toward the emergency entrance and to the ambulance area where the vehicles were parked. Theran Ward was a Justice of the Peace for Dallas County and this arrangement evidently seemed to satisfy the immediate legal need in the minds of the local authorities. In any event, it was quite clear that the President was already inside of the sealed casket and the federal agents were not about to stop their moving the casket of the deceased President's remains out of the hospital for anyone.

We finally managed to get the casket around the people standing in the hallway glaring at us. Our entourage was allowed to pass, but you could see the fury in everyone's faces that the federal men had won the fight. I headed toward the emergency doorway where our ambulance was parked, and where Mr. O'Neal had also parked his brand new 1964 Cadillac hearse.

Hearses are manufactured in a variety of auto-body styles. In limousine style hearses, the rear casket compartment had glass windows on all sides much like a conventional station wagon. These windowed panels gave the vehicle an ambulance look, especially if the vehicle was white and had white drapes in those rear windows. The hearse was parked in the ambulance bay to our extreme left with the rear door facing toward the hospital doorway.

I was approaching the emergency entrance doorway when I immediately stopped in my tracks, thereby stopping the flow of the casket and its escorts behind me. There were about four hundred people outside surrounding the emergency entrance and parking lot of the hospital, and the anxiety of the crowd was evident.

The Secret Service agent urgently demanded, "Come on, let's go!" as he was clearly more than a little bit anxious to get the casket with the President out of the hospital before someone changed their mind about letting us go.

However, I was alarmed because of all of the tension and heightened sense of security in most everyone anywhere around the place. Outside the emergency department, the exterior of the hospital was teaming with all manner of armed personnel just a heartbeat from drawing their weapon, and I was truthfully concerned for my personal safety. Everyone, everywhere, just seemed to be all too ready to draw his or her weapons on each other and a crowd that was obviously just barely under control.

Anxiously, I replied, "I ain't going first. I don't want to get shot."

The Secret Service agent hurriedly pushed by me and went out the door ahead of me and I more or less followed right behind him headed to the rear door of the hearse with the casket.

I jerked opened the rear door of the hearse and began to load the casket. It was pushed from the dolly onto what we call a casket table, a set of rollers that are mounted almost flush with the floor. These casket tables are also most often fitted with a set of pegs or pins that fit into slots or holes in metal tracks that are inset in the floor or casket table of the hearse. These pins or pegs are adjustable and they are intended to prevent the caskets from moving or rolling around while the vehicle is in motion.

I had begun loading the casket onto the rollers when Mrs. Kennedy informed me that she wanted to ride in the rear of the car with the casket. The hearse was a multipurpose vehicle as it could be made to serve as an transfer ambulance. As such, it was equipped with a rear compartment attendant's seat which was ultimately occupied by Mrs. Kennedy on the ride back out to Air Force One at Love Field.

I was concerned about Mrs. Kennedy riding in the back, even if she was seated to one side, because there was the risk that she could be hurt if the head and foot end pegs did not stabilize the casket as planned. I cautioned her about the danger of the casket shifting.

However, she was adamant, saying, "I don't care. I'm going to ride back there anyway."

We walked around to the side of the vehicle and I opened the rear right door adjacent to the attendant's folding jump seat. I adjusted the seat and pointed out a deep well just inside the door that she would have to step into in order to enter the vehicle. While we stood inside the open car door, I gently grasped Mrs. Kennedy's right forearm near her elbow to assist her into the car. At that time, as I still had her by the arm, a Secret Service agent grabbed me by my arm and spinning me around slammed me back and into the open car door.

Mrs. Kennedy turned angrily and immediately said to this agent, "You leave that young man alone! He's the only gentlemen I've met since I've been here."

The agent instantly backed off, and surprised, I managed to reply with, "Thank you Ma'am" as I helped her into the jump seat and closed the door.

As soon as the door closed, three Secret Service agents jumped into the front seat of the hearse and three more Secret Service agents jumped into the back of the hearse to hold the casket in place. Then the car started to roll away from the emergency ramp and onto the hospital driveway.

We were just left standing there. Mr. O'Neal looked at me and declared, "God damn, Al. That SOB done stole my hearse! Let's get in your ambulance and chase them down!"

Peanuts, Mr. O'Neal and I jumped into my ambulance. Mr. O'Neal was riding shotgun and Peanuts in the attendant's jump seat in the back as I sped out of the ambulance bay to try and catch up with the motorcade that was heading North on Harry Hines Boulevard, out to Love Field and to Air Force One.

Mr. O'Neal shouted, "Put on them red lights and siren and let's catch them SOBs! I want to get my hearse back!"

In obedience to his orders I drove out of the Parkland Memorial Hospital lot at Code 3, racing to catch up to the hearse we could see positioned immediately behind the official group of vehicles heading toward Love Field.

At about the time I fell in behind the last car, the Dallas Police 2-way radio carried the following message, "Would the escort on Hines cut your sirens. The escort on Hines cut your sirens, cut your sirens."

I immediately reached over and turned off the siren allowing conversation in the car. First thing out of Peg O'Neal's mouth was, "those SOBs better not mess up my car."

Love Field

Chapter 12

What had been a noisy, disorganized swarm of demanding reporters and gruff, commanding police had somehow become a quietly sobbing, motionless crowd. The plane carrying the body of our slain President was leaving Dallas.

W e traveled north on Harry Hines Boulevard to Mockingbird Lane and then east on Mockingbird Lane to Cedar Springs Road before going north again to Love Field Airport. We used an airport service road around to the east concourse that intersects with Aviation Drive, then drove directly out to where Air Force One was parked on the tarmac.

The Dallas Police Department had positioned a string of patrol cars as a barrier to control the flow of people and vehicles into the area. Shortly after 2 o'clock, we entered the restricted area, and were made aware there was a command post setup and were told to go to that area.

When we pulled up to the command post, Mr. O'Neal directed me to, "Drive on out there to where the plane is so we can get my hearse."

However, we were stopped by a police officer who said, "Just stand by until Air Force One has left, and we'll bring your hearse to you."

I parked the ambulance and the three of us walked towards the command post. There was no building, or even tent; there was just a large group of people congregated around a smaller number of dignitaries. Most of the group were news people, yelling out questions, scrambling and pushing each other trying to get close to anyone who might talk to them.

Over on the side, there was a chain link fence. When the Kennedys arrived at Love Field earlier that day that is where people from Dallas had gathered to welcome them. The people of Dallas were there again, there this time to say goodbye to a slain but still much loved President and First Lady.

Immediately, we looked over to Air Force One and the hearse holding the body of President Kennedy. As Peanuts and I stood on the tarmac looking at Air Force One about 300 feet away, I could easily see lots of men in suits, and several in blue uniforms. After just a few moments, someone walked over to the now stopped hearse and opened the car door so Mrs. Kennedy could get out.

Then, men I believed to be Secret Service agents walked to the rear of the vehicle and opened the rear compartment door of the hearse. The milling crowds froze in place as the casket holding the body of President Kennedy was slowly drawn from the hearse.

That bronze casket was heavy, at least 400 pounds when empty, so those men had a heavy burden. Unfortunately, no one had thought ahead and there was no casket cart or church truck on which to place it; and there was no way the men would be as disrespectful as to put it on the ground. That left them no choice but to try to get in the plane while carrying the heavy casket by hand.

We watched as they struggled to carry that solid bronze casket up the passenger ramp that was stationed at the aircraft's rear left hand side passenger door. The men staggered as they tilted the casket and, halfway up it looked like they almost dropped it. Two crewmembers promptly came down the steps and tried to help.

By the time the men finally got it to the top, the group of Dallas citizens behind the fence and the newsmen and dignitaries at the command post where unable to contain their tears. The experience was surreal. Jacqueline Kennedy stood near the passenger ramp as the casket was lifted up and into the rear of the plane. She then climbed up the steps, right behind those who were carrying the casket. The casket eventually disappeared into the plane, followed by Mrs. Kennedy. That was the last time that Peanuts, Mr. O'Neal or I ever saw that bronze casket.

About 15 minutes went by; during that time, the crowd at the command post became more animated. Peanuts and I hung back from the mob of noisy men, but Peg O'Neal just acted like the affable businessman he always was. With his Kool cigarette hanging from his lips he merged with the crowd, limply shaking hands, introducing himself as if he was at a business gathering and he was networking for clients.

News reporters were out there from several news stations. They eventually noticed Peanuts and I and of course they all wanted interviews. As we were busy being interrogated on the tarmac, Judge Sarah T. Hughes arrived. She entered the area driving at a high rate of speed in her blue, 1950s Dodge DeSoto sedan. She sped up to the gate at the command post, slammed on her brakes and slid to a stop with the gravel flying. The Dallas Police officers who were on hand had all scattered from in front of her car in fear for their lives.

In disbelief, I muttered, "That crazy woman!" Everyone there knew to watch out for her erratic driving. She was a notoriously bad driver, and the circumstances appeared to have had no impact on her driving habits.

Sarah Hughes' accomplishments during her many years on the bench and her involvement in Democratic Party politics were rewarded in October 1961 when President Kennedy appointed her the first woman to serve as United States District Judge for the Northern District of Texas. Judge Hughes explained her appearance by stating she had been summoned to swear Vice President Johnson into the office of President.

The Dallas Police cleared the way for her out onto the tarmac and she drove out to a point very close to where the presidential jet was sitting and brazenly parked her big DeSoto out there on the tarmac. She disappeared into the aircraft for about 30 minutes. After Judge Hughes completed the swearing in ceremony, she returned to her car and drove off.

Soon a member of the Secret Service brought Mr. O'Neal's Cadillac hearse to us at the command post, and then we watched Air Force One taxi out onto the runway preparing for take off for Washington, DC. As I watched the plane leave, I had a really empty feeling inside of me. As the plane made its way into flight, you could not hear any sound other than the sound of that airplane, the almost lonesome whine of the jet engines.

The crowd of news people and all of the spectators were silent, literally speechless. The reporters and spectators who were close enough for me to see were wiping their eyes of tears. I did my share of crying too, I felt very, very empty inside and sad; I was suddenly very much aware that I loved both John and Jacqueline Kennedy.

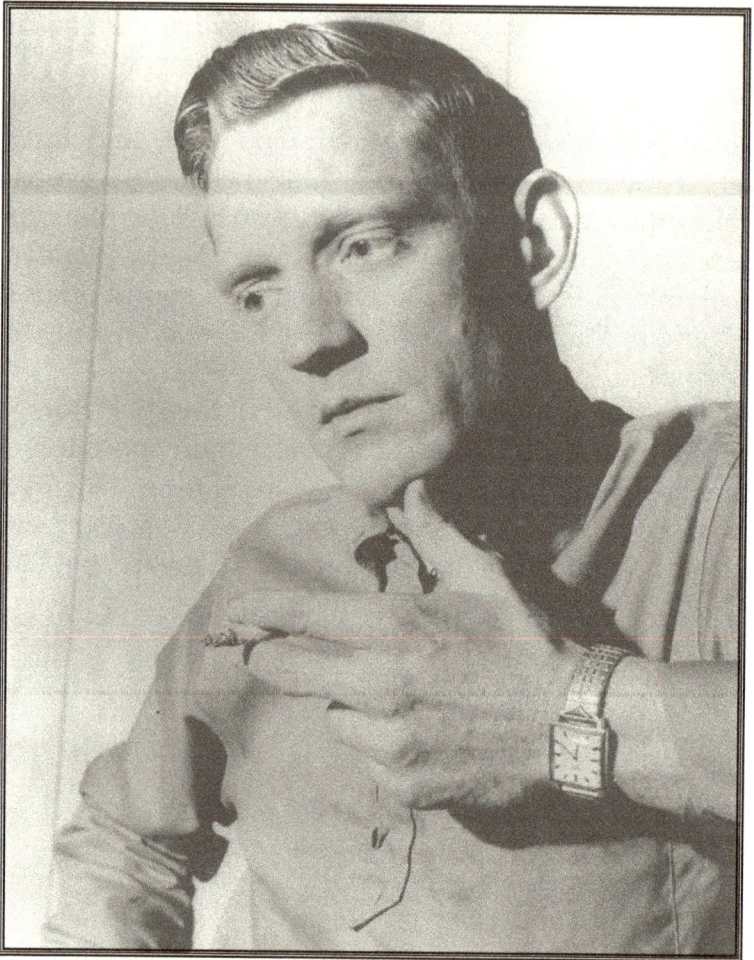

News Service Photo of Aubrey Rike taken the early evening (about 6:20 p.m.) of Friday November 22, 1963 at the Dallas Offices of the Associated Press. This photo was used in newspapers across the nation in articles on the assassination. (AP/The Associated Press)

Texas newspaper photo showing the arrival of President and Mrs. Kennedy arriving at Love Field. Governor John Connally and wife Nellie are in the doorway. November 22, 1963. (Source unavailable)

Parkland Emergency entrance. Secret Service Agents secure the vehicle roof back on the presidential limousine. Note the bucket on ground between the agent & the helmeted officer. It was at this approximate interval of time that Aubrey & Peanuts had placed their redressed gurney back into their ambulance (at left). (White House Photographer Cecil Stoughton)

Peanuts outside of the emergency room entrance at Parkland Hospital.
Aubrey is out of view but is standing next to Peanuts. The ambulance
is the white vehicle to the left in the photos. (*Dallas Times Herald*
Collection/The Sixth Floor Museum at Dealey Plaza)

Aubrey and Peanuts watch as Secret Service and Kennedy Staffers enter Parkland Hospital. Assistant Presidential Press Secretary Malcolm Kilduff has just passed behind Aubrey. Kilduff will shortly hold a press conference where he will announce the death of President John Kennedy. (*Dallas Times Herald* Collection/The Sixth Floor Museum at Dealey Plaza)

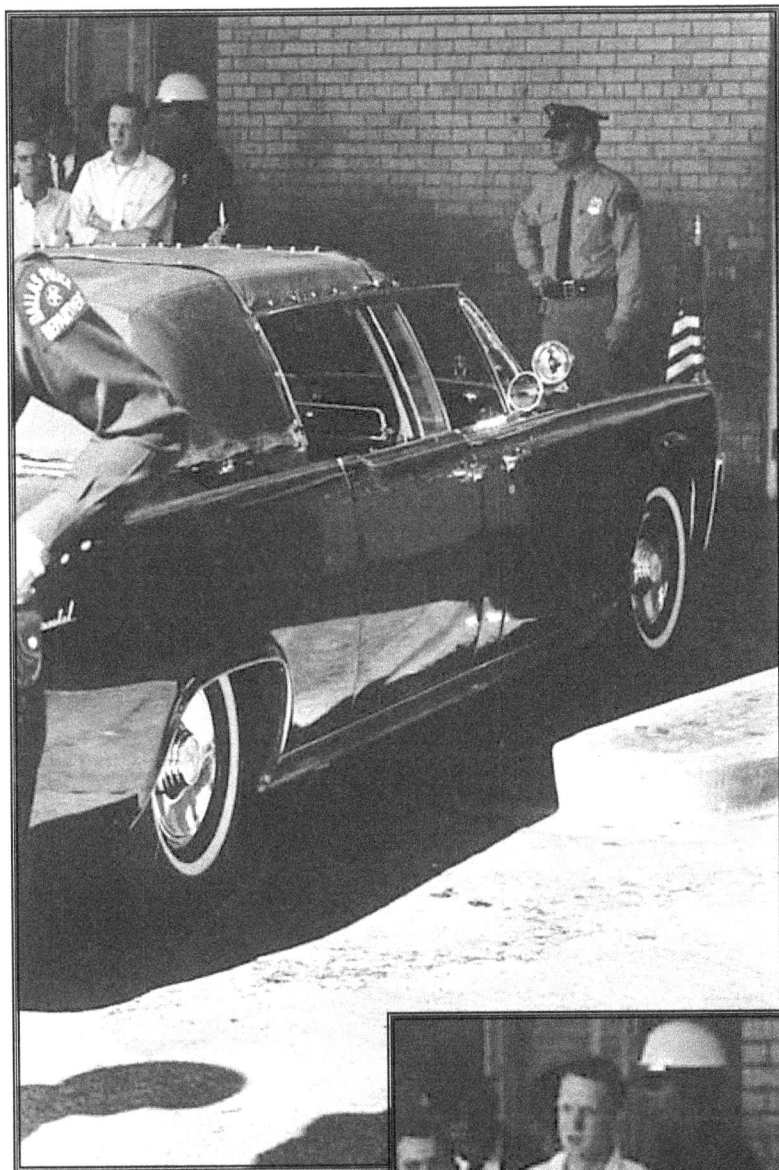

Peanuts and Aubrey standing at the Parkland emergency entrance. (Photographer Unknown)

Aubrey assisting with the bronze coffin. (*Dallas Times Herald* Collection/
The Sixth Floor Museum at Dealey Plaza)

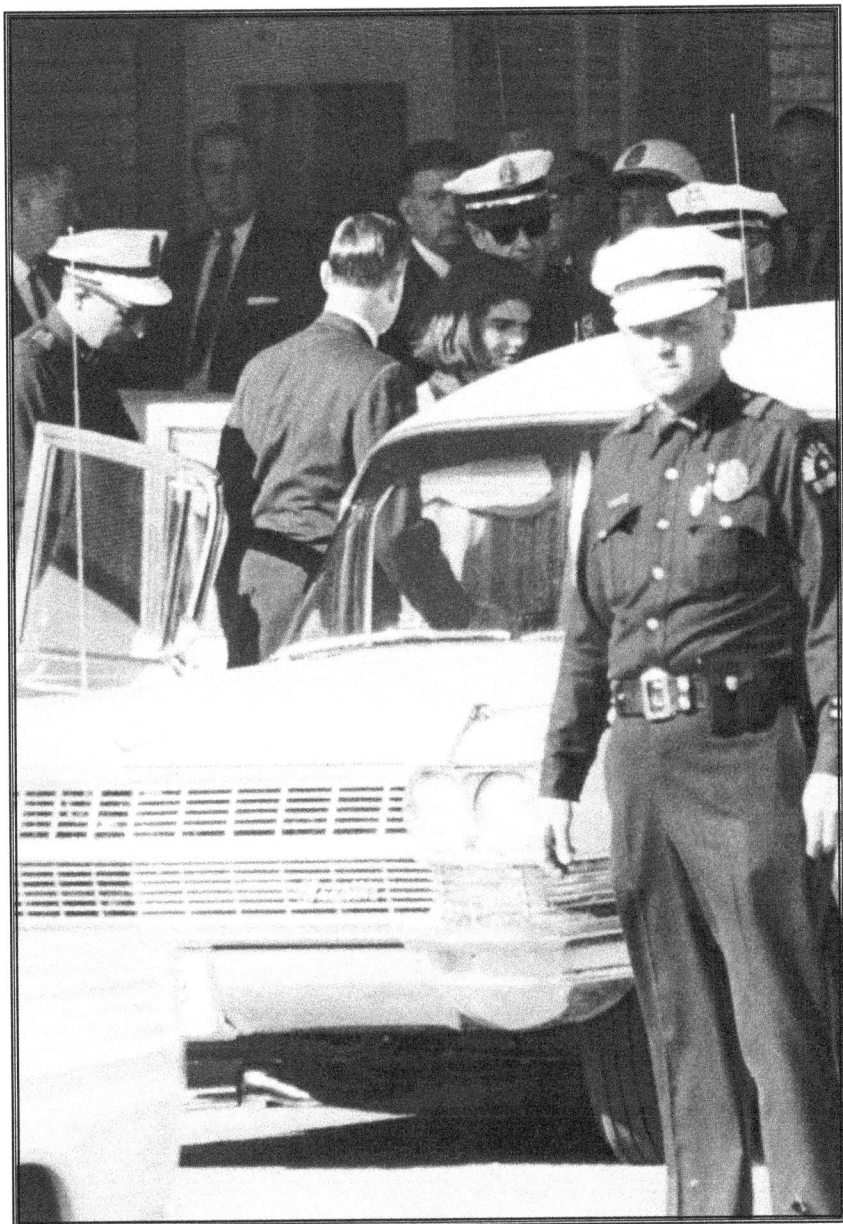

Mrs. Kennedy stands at the rear right passenger side door of Mr. O'Neal's hearse . Aubrey Rike is out of our view as he prepares the attendant's seat for Mrs. Kennedy's use. (*The Dallas Morning News*)

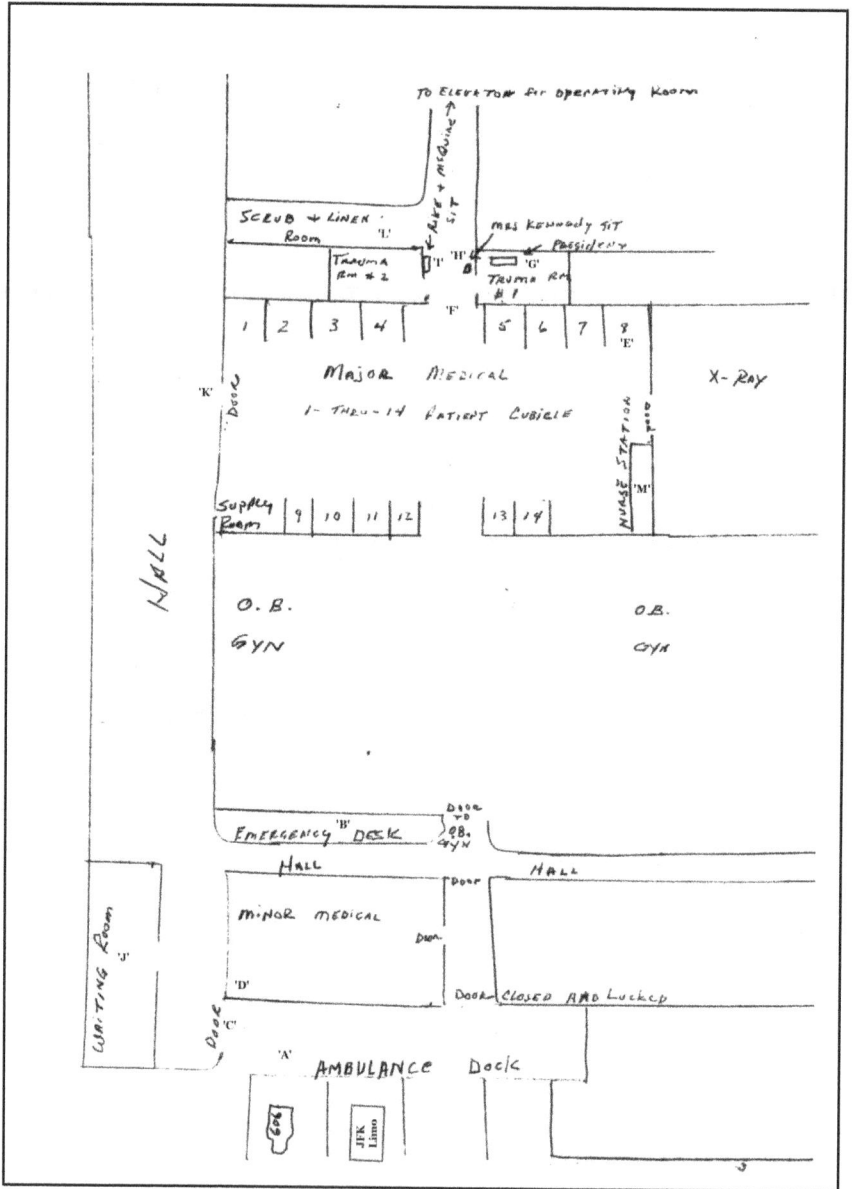

Aubrey's drawing of floor plan of Parkland Memorial Hospital's emergency department as it was in November 1963. (A. Rike, 2006)

PARKLAND MEMORIAL HOSPITAL:
Emergency Department Floor Plan

A. Emergency Entrance & Ambulance Bays/Docks & Location of ambulance #606. The presidential limo JFK limo had been parked immediately beside #606.

B. Emergency Desk where Aubrey & 'Peanuts' were approached by Secret Service agents seeking gurneys.

C. Emergency Entrance doorway used to bring LBJ, JBC & JFK into the emergency area.

D. Minor Medicine where Vice President Lyndon Johnson was sequestered during hospital ordeal.

E. Major Medicine stall #8 where Aubrey & 'Peanuts' placed the epileptic seizure patient.

F. Trauma Room corridor.

G. Trauma Room 1 where President Kennedy was treated, expired & casketed for repatriation to Washington, DC.

H. Mrs. Jacqueline Kennedy location.

I. Aubrey & Peanuts' location.

J. Waiting Room & cigarette vending machine where Aubrey bought cigarettes under police & Secret Service supervision.

K. Doorway into Major Medicine where altercation between Secret Service agents & FBI agent transpired.

L. Scrub Room where Aubrey obtained water moistened towel for Mrs. Kennedy to clean herself off with.

M. Nursing Station where Aubrey phoned Mr. O'Neal to bring a casket for President Kennedy & from where he noticed that the epileptic was no longer in stall #8.

Meet the Press

Chapter 13

By the time I had finished the three interviews, I have to admit I had gotten a swelled head. Imagine, in just a few hours I had been interviewed by local news reporters, done a television interview and spoken with the famous Walter Cronkite.

Once the presidential plane was out of sight people began to slowly make their way to their vehicles and leave Love Field. Mr. O'Neal drove away in the hearse headed toward the funeral home. Once there, he felt the need to formally acknowledge what had happened. He placed a brief obituary notice in the local papers to run on Saturday, November 23, 1963. Noticeably missing were a number of names of the members of the family of President Kennedy, the obituary notice read:

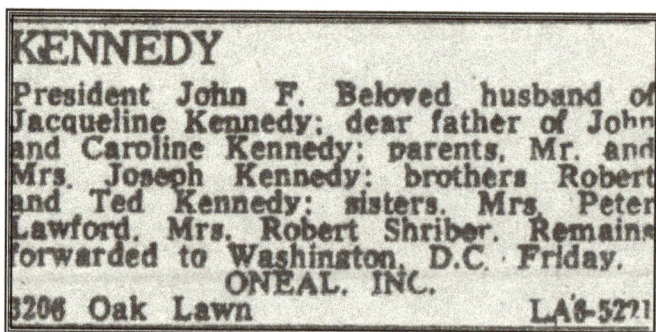

> **KENNEDY**
> President John F. Beloved husband of Jacqueline Kennedy; dear father of John and Caroline Kennedy; parents, Mr. and Mrs. Joseph Kennedy; brothers Robert and Ted Kennedy; sisters, Mrs. Peter Lawford, Mrs. Robert Shriber. Remains forwarded to Washington, D.C. Friday.
> ONEAL, INC.
> 3206 Oak Lawn   LA8-5271

Peanuts and I returned to ambulance 606 and checked back on the air with the O'Neal dispatcher indicating we were once again available for ambulance calls. Then we made our way back to the funeral home. Minutes after our return, Peanuts and I received a phone call from WFAA Television in Dallas. They were asking Peanuts and me to come down to the station for a television interview.

The WFAA TV Station was located next to the Dallas Morning News building just off South Houston Street and about three blocks south of Dealey Plaza where the assassination had happened. I did not anticipate the reaction of the press or news crews to our involvement with the body after the assassination.

WFAA did a live interview with Peanuts and I in their studio that was broadcast over the ABC national network and a second one that was taped for local showing at a later time. There was a bunch of people present as the station employees gathered around to watch and listen to the interview with us. One of the people there happened to notice the blood that was still on my shirtsleeve and offered me fifty dollars for the shirt. Fifty dollars was a lot of money in those days, in fact it was more than a week's salary for me. I had only paid about six dollars for the shirt in the first place, but I refused the offer outright.

As we were finishing the taped interview, someone told me that Walter Cronkite had called the station and wanted to conduct a five-minute telephone interview with me. The telephone was in a nearby office, so I left the group to do the interview. This of course, did nothing to subdue my normally overconfident attitude.

After I left the WFAA TV station, I went home quickly to change my shirt, just throwing the one tainted with the President's blood in the hamper, and since I was still on duty, I went back to the funeral home. Later, Glenda would wash the bloody garment has she had so many others over the years, with no thought to whose blood had stained my shirt. Soon after I arrived, I was summoned to Mr. O'Neal's office in the front of the building to speak with someone on the phone.

Meet the FBI

Chapter 14

When you are nervous or afraid, it is sometimes easier to conceal your apprehension with bold behavior. Of course, being just twenty-five can also give you inappropriate daring. Therefore, smarting off to the FBI seemed like just the thing to do.

I completed my telephone conversation and as I sat there at the big desk of Mr. O'Neal, the second line on the telephone rang. I answered it and the caller was a man who identified himself as an FBI Agent. He told me that he wanted me, and my assistant, to come down to their office and that he wanted to talk to me.

Feeling sassy and safe on my own turf, I smarted off and said, "If you want to talk to me, you'll have to come out to my office." I guess I had gotten to feeling somewhat important what with being sought out by Walter Cronkite for an interview and all.

About ten minutes later, I was still talking on the phone at Mr. O'Neal's desk. I had my feet crossed and my legs propped up on the desktop, me being the new big shot and all. Then I heard it. Ka-Boom! The FBI men had arrived, and they had made quite an entrance. The funeral home had a set of double doors on the main front entryway into the building and when the FBI agents arrived, they knocked both of the doors wide open with a kick or something like it. The feet came off the desk, immediately.

One of the agents held a folder in his hand, and the other flashed something about the size of a business card that had the letters FBI in large black letters on it. They never did produce an actual badge or other official looking credentials for me that I remember seeing.

They looked around scanning the room quickly, and then one of them barked, "Where is that other little skinny boy that was with you?"

I lazily replied, "Oh, you talking about Peanuts?"

The FBI agent snapped, "I don't know his name. Just tell him to get his skinny ass in here!"

I mischievously called upstairs on the intercom and told Peanuts that he had "company" that wanted to see him. Peanuts came down from upstairs within seconds of my call to him and the FBI agent growled to Peanuts and I, "Y'all get your skinny asses out into the car."

I called upstairs to the dispatcher and let him know that we had to go downtown with some men and that we would be out of service. The FBI men had parked their car in a fire zone directly in front of O'Neal's on Oak Lawn, which of course was a no parking zone. I could not resist and once again smarted off saying, "I guess y'all know that you're in a no parking zone."

They simply snarled, "Get in the car!"

Peanuts and I were driven by the FBI Agents down to the Dallas FBI office. Once there, they took us into an office where yet another man was seated behind a big desk. He told us to sit down.

I arrogantly asked, "Where?"

In response, an FBI agent aggressively "helped" me into the chair with a forcible thrust. After that, I did not pay any attention to who else was there, who the FBI agents were, or anything. I knew where the line had been drawn and I was dangerously close to stepping over it with dire consequences. I guess you could say I was in shock, and at just twenty-five, suddenly intimidated by the dark suits and stern faces of older men who were not in the mood for any of my shenanigans.

After a short and sweet interview with the FBI agents present, the man behind the desk warned, "Keep your f***ing mouths shut or we will shut them for you." Then he ordered, "Get out of here."

When I asked him if they were going to drive us back to the funeral home, he retorted, "Take a f***ing bus back."

In another office, we used one of the FBI telephones to call Mr. O'Neal. I told him to send someone to pick us up and he sent a limousine. Feeling the worst was over, I smarted off one last time when the limousine arrived saying to the FBI agents standing with us, "If any of y'all need a ride, I've got my limousine outside."

Back at O'Neals

Chapter 15

The only thing that I can compare it to would be like spending an exciting day at a fair or something that totally absorbs you and then getting home to nothing. Peanuts and I had been in the middle of something huge, like the middle of a storm, a vortex and then we were suddenly left in a vacuum.

P eanuts and I rode back to the O'Neal's in the funeral home's limousine. Once there we received a call from the Associated Press. They wanted to do an interview with both of us and they wanted us at their offices as soon as we could get there.

Ignoring the freshly received instructions of the FBI, Peanuts and I got in one of the O'Neal ambulances and we drove ourselves down to the Associated Press Offices there in downtown Dallas and did an interview with them. My photograph was taken while I was in their offices. That particular photo would end up being used in a number of newspaper articles on the assassination locally and elsewhere across the country. We never heard from the FBI about this obvious act of flagrant disobedience to their orders.

Naturally everyone on the funeral home staff back at O'Neal's were concerned and curious to learn from us what had gone on throughout the day, and we related the story of our day's activities as best as we could. Once we had told our stories, we remained on duty until 8 AM the next morning, mostly upstairs in the funeral home watching television.

Naturally, the only programs on any of three channels that we could get were all about the assassination.

It was while watching television that I learned of the shooting death of Dallas Policeman JD Tippit. The news about JD was quite upsetting for me personally, because I had actually known him for a couple of years.

I met JD about 1960, while still employed by the Ambulance Service Company. He had worked patrol duty in south Oak Cliff where I responded to emergency calls we both worked. Sometimes we would meet for lunch or for a quick break when we were on duty at the same time. We became friends and I visited his house once over on Glencairn, which was in Oak Cliff and not that far from where Glenda and I lived.

JD was a nice person and a good, decent and honorable public servant; he was proud to be a police officer for the City of Dallas. He was polite, honest, and always willing to help other people. He talked about his wife Marie and his three children often; he clearly loved his family.

Dallas Police Officer JD Tippit was laid to rest at Laurel Land Cemetery located at the corner of the R. L. Thornton Freeway and Laurel Land Road East. The mortuary establishment of Dudley M. Hughes Funeral Home handled the funeral arrangements.

They placed the following obituary notice in the local papers that appeared on the same day as the one for President Kennedy:

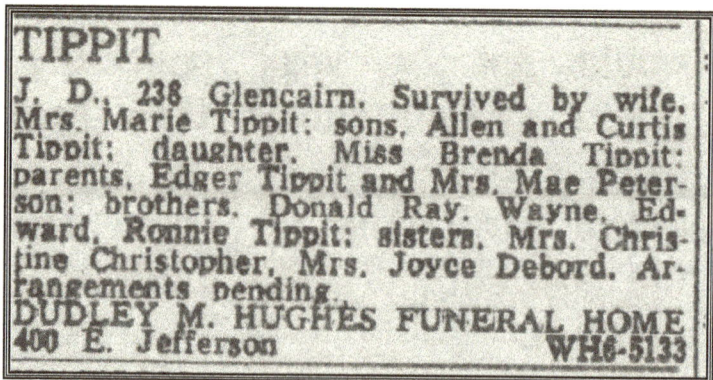

TIPPIT

J. D., 238 Glencairn. Survived by wife, Mrs. Marie Tippit; sons, Allen and Curtis Tippit; daughter, Miss Brenda Tippit; parents, Edger Tippit and Mrs. Mae Peterson; brothers, Donald Ray, Wayne, Edward, Ronnie Tippit; sisters, Mrs. Christine Christopher, Mrs. Joyce Debord. Arrangements pending.
DUDLEY M. HUGHES FUNERAL HOME
400 E. Jefferson   WH6-5133

After hearing about my friend JD, I had endured enough television news for the day, but there was nothing else to do. It was an extremely quiet afternoon and night; in fact, we had no other calls on our shift at all. There was hardly any traffic on the streets, and all businesses were closed as a result of the death of the President. There was just nothing moving anywhere in the entire city of Dallas that night.

About 8 o'clock in the evening, Peanuts and I realized we had not eaten, so we walked across Oak Lawn Avenue from the funeral home to the Waffle House for dinner. Although it was the only place that was still open at that hour, the place was completely empty other than us, and of course whoever happened to be working there. We both ordered grilled cheese sandwiches and vanilla malts, thinking ourselves hungry. Yet, when the food was served, neither of us had an appetite and sampled only a bite or two.

It was really quite strange, because neither one of us had spoken a word, other than what we had said to the waitress to place our order, nor had we eaten anything since breakfast. We were both just very quiet. We had been living on pure adrenalin all day and then when everything had finally quieted down, everything inside of our bodies, our nerves, our emotions and everything within us just began to fall; we were crashing physically and emotionally.

The only thing that I can compare it to would be like spending an exciting day at a fair or something that totally absorbs you mentally and physically and then getting home to nothing. Peanuts and I had been in the middle of something huge like the middle of a storm, a whirling vortex of people, and emotion. Then we suddenly found ourselves in a vacuum.

I actually felt like I had lost a close family member. I know that I sincerely admired and loved President Kennedy, and I could not help but feel deep concern for Mrs. Kennedy. She had no relatives, no friends, no one to lean on anywhere in Dallas to help her through this horrific day.

I looked up at Peanuts at about the same time that he looked up at me; I said, "I'm goin'."

Silently we rose, leaving our food, and walked back over Oak Lawn to the funeral home. Peanuts went upstairs to where we normally spent our time. I headed to the casket selection room. I went inside the room, closed the door behind me and wept uncontrollably.

I was probably in there for at least twenty minutes or maybe a bit more. I finally slipped outside to get some badly needed air to try to revive myself. I was definitely not up to watching anything on the television, especially as I knew all stations would be focusing on the events of that day in Dallas, and I could not relive that again just now.

I got off work at 8AM Saturday morning and drove to the Baker Hotel in downtown Dallas where I had promised a news reporter I would tape an interview with him. Once the interview was over, I went home to our place in Oak Cliff. Glenda was working, so I went to bed and I slept most of the day away.

Glenda's Story

Chapter 16

He was so openly distraught he could not speak a word for several minutes. He still has those moments when describing that day in November, even after all these years. When asked if the assassination changed him, he always says no; but I know the truth, and when I am asked, I shake my head yes, my face grim with memory.

I was working as a bookkeeper for the Lance snack foods the morning the President and Mrs. Kennedy were in Dallas. My co-workers and I were talking about how we wished the motorcade that was moving through Dallas had been scheduled to pass in front of our building; our third floor office would have given us a prefect viewing position. We hadn't gone to lunch yet, if they had been scheduled close to our building, perhaps we might have even been able to go down to the street for a close look at the President and his wife known affectionately as Jackie.

Then the intercom for the building began to crackle, hinting a message was about to be delivered. The somber voice gave the sad news; President Kennedy had been shot and killed. There was no time for a reaction, immediately the only telephone in the room began to ring, and the secretary motioned it was for me.

This was unusual as I seldom received telephone calls. Aubrey would call just before the end of my workday if he was working a 24-hour shift and sleeping at the job; other that that no one ever called me at work.

I said "Hello?" and a brisk, emotionless voice started talking rapidly. He identified himself by name, but when he said, "FBI agent," everything he had said previous to that was lost.

"We have your husband..." My mind raced, thinking, *What do you mean you have my husband?*

"Do you know the President is dead?" he quickly inquired, subtly insinuating Aubrey was in some way involved.

"Yes," I warily replied, while silently wondering, *What does that have to do with Aubrey?*

While hardly allowing time for me to respond, he gruffly continued. "You need to keep your mouth shut, do you understand?"

"Yes" I managed; then I heard a click. He had hung up. I had no time to ask anything and had no answers for the questions running through my mind. *What is going on? Who did he say he was?*

As I replaced the receiver, the woman I normally went to lunch with was approaching me, her eyes questioning me. I must have looked as scared as I felt. Less than five seconds had passed and my life was changed.

"Are you ok? What's happened?" She ask, clearly worried about me.

"I can't tell you now, but I'll tell you later," I promised.

I had all sorts of things going through my mind: who called me, where was Aubrey, what did he have to do with the assassination of the President, how did they know my name and how did they find me?

At lunch, I revealed everything; that phone call was just too frightening and too disturbing to be silent. When we returned from lunch I reluctantly told my other co-workers what had happened. However, by that time the local news was revealing more than the phone call had told me. We talked about what I could possibly do to find Aubrey.

They unsuccessfully tried to reassure me by saying if anything bad had actually happened, Aubrey would have called me himself; and every time the telephone rang, one of them would suggest he was calling, but frighteningly, it was not. The remainder of the day was filled with incessant speculation about what had happened, and what part Aubrey might have played in the aftermath of the assassination.

I finished out the afternoon at work, and rode the bus home physically drained and emotionally exhausted. Like thousands of others, I turned on the television, completely mesmerized by the news reports following the assassination of President Kennedy. I did not hear from Aubrey at all; however, his brother, Ricky did.

When I answered, his first words were "How does it feel to have your husband be a celebrity?"

I retorted, "I didn't know he was!" Then we both laughed. That laughter was a respite from the emotional stress that had been slowly building all day. The remainder of that conversation was like every other I had that day, the telephone call from the mystery FBI agent, the fact that the President was shot and killed, and my concern over the lack of communication with Aubrey.

I had not heard from Aubrey, and no matter how many times I told myself he was all right, I was worried. Ricky tried to alleviate my fear by insisting Aubrey was okay, after all, he had been on radio and television and was obviously being hounded by the media. Even after I told him about receiving the telephone call from the FBI agent at work, he said that he did not think there was any reason to be worried. Ricky had spoken with him, Aubrey was fine and was probably just too busy being questioned and interviewed to have an opportunity or time to call me.

The next day at work was like déjà vu; the assassination dominated every conversation. The name Aubrey Rike had made the news and people who worked in the building came to the office on the third floor to ask me questions, some because they knew some and me, and some because they wondered if the handsome young ambulance driver on the television with the same last name was somehow related to me.

The women in the office and I chattered nonstop about the television reports on the evening news; everything that had happened was being rehashed and analyzed on every television station offered. I had an overwhelmingly sinister feeling all day, but I was not really scared, I guess you could say I was worried more than afraid.

I was incredibly relieved when the day was over and Aubrey picked me up from work to bring me home. He told me everything that had happened; related seeing the motorcade, being at Parkland, and meeting Mrs. Kennedy. He discussed the FBI, all the news interviews, what people had asked him pertaining to the assassination, and finally, how he felt about everything. He was saddened because President Kennedy had been assassinated, but excited about being involved. He was overwhelmed with emotion when talking about some of the experiences he had.

When Aubrey was telling me about the assassination and being in the trauma room with Mrs. Kennedy, he said she was one of the most beautiful women he had been around, even with what she had been through that day. He thought she had a demeanor about her that presented an air of sophistication and dignity, in spite of the fact that she was sitting on a folding chair outside a room where her dead husband lay. Aubrey said she remained calm and composed, although at times he recognized turmoil and sheer terror in her eyes, as if she were silently asking, *Why?* and *What Next?*

Aubrey was concerned because while he was with her, no one ever approached her to offer comfort or even sit with her. Especially harsh in his eyes were the Secret Service agents and FBI agents that evidently knew her, yet were so concerned with the event that had taken place that they were not even cordial to her, and at moments were inexplicably rude.

When Aubrey began telling me about Mrs. Kennedy taking off her wedding ring and putting it on her dead husband's finger, revealing in detail what he did to help her, my heart was suddenly heavy in my chest and tears came to my eyes. Aubrey became very emotional, tears glistened in his eyes and at times, he was so openly distraught he could not speak a word for several minutes. He still has those moments when describing that day in November, even after all these years. When asked if the assassination changed him, he always says no; but I know the truth, and when I am asked, I shake my head yes, my face grim with memory.

For weeks after President Kennedy's funeral, Aubrey was still called for questioning and interviews with radio correspondents, television newsmen and newspaper journalists. Over the years, I have watched him tell his story: at JFK Lancer's November in Dallas Conferences, during interviews with countless individuals, a number of times for American and British television and twice at speaking engagements in Canada arranged by Colin McSween.

I have sat in the audience of small community group meetings and educational seminars such as for Mark Taylor's high school students. I listen to his quiet soft voice as he reminisces about Mrs. Kennedy and Trauma Room 1. However, the most frequent venue has been in private moments as I listened in the dark as we lay in bed. The story has never changed; it may have varied in detail or focus, but it has never changed. Nor has my admiration for my husband.

Looking Back

Chapter 17

I am not the same daring young man who raced daringly around the streets of Dallas, lights flashing and sirens blaring. Furthermore, I have had many years to look back on that day and wonder if I did the best I could.

In the years following the assassination of President Kennedy, Peg O'Neal tried a number of times to retrieve his solid bronze casket from the government. In fact, he made three separate trips back and forth to Washington, DC in those efforts.

Each time I picked Mr. O'Neal up at Love Field after his return flights from Washington home to Dallas, the first thing he would always say to me was, "Those sons of bitches won't let me have my damned casket back."

In June 1999, the National Archives released documents indicating the bronze casket, which had once held President Kennedy's body, was sunk off the Delaware coast, in more than 9,000 feet of water in an abandoned military dumpsite. The documents indicated that the President's brother, Robert Kennedy, insisted that the coffin be disposed of to prevent it from becoming an object of morbid curiosity.

Apparently, the coffin was loaded with sandbags and perforated with holes after being taken from the basement of the National Archives building in downtown Washington, and then dumped from an Air Force C-130 into the Atlantic Ocean at 10 a.m. on February 18, 1966. The documents also explained the bronze casket had been replaced because it was damaged. Damaged or not, Mr. O'Neal wanted it back, but that was never going to happen.

I left the employ of Mr. O'Neal in 1964 and got a job with the Superior Coach Company. The Superior Coach Company had their headquarters in Lima, Ohio where they manufactured custom-built ambulances, hearses and limousines. I drove the new vehicles from their plant in Lima to their lot in Dallas. Following that, I worked from about 1965 until 1967 for a bakery company. My duties there were to deliver baked goods to various stores all over the Dallas area.

My next career would fulfill my youthful dreams when I applied to the Highland Park Police Department and was hired in 1967. Highland Park is an "Old Money," extremely wealthy district in Dallas; it's beautiful, with handsome tree lined streets, parks, and huge mansions and vast estates. It is situated to the North East of Love Field Airport, and just beyond the area known as White Rock. I stayed with the Highland Park Police Department for over 26 years until when as a Sergeant, I retired.

In those later years, I gained experience both as a police officer and in fighting fires while serving with the Highland Park Police Department. I followed my career as a city police officer with one as a sheriff's deputy, working for ten years with the Dallas County Sheriff's Department whose offices are located at Dealey Plaza in downtown Dallas. In total, I devoted thirty-six years of my life to the law enforcement profession.

My years with the Highland Park Police included VIP Security and Protection Service responsibilities. This work had me serving a number of my nation's presidents as well as visiting foreign heads of state whenever their travels brought them to Dallas, Texas. Some of these VIPs for whom I provided security detail services for included Presidents Richard Nixon, Gerald Ford, Ronald Reagan, and George H. W. Bush, as well as British Prime Minister Margaret Thatcher and many others, including former U.S. First Lady Mamie D. Eisenhower.

These visiting heads of state were billeted in some of the finest mansions in Highland Park. Many visits included games of golf at an area golf and country club in which I was also on official security duty. I served in security on one of those golf games in which the players were President Gerald Ford & comedian Bob Hope.

During my years with the Highland Park Police Department, I also met a number of other notable personalities and characters, including the infamous John Hinckley Jr., to whom I had the distinction of being the police officer who gave him his first traffic ticket. This young fellow, some years later, would make his way into the history pages as the man who attempted to assassinate U.S. President Ronald Reagan in Washington, DC in March 1981.

During the years since then, I have become acquainted with many people who were conducting investigations into the Kennedy Assassination. Among these were Jim Garrison District Attorney in the late 1960s of Orleans Parish in New Orleans, Louisiana, author David S. Lifton of Los Angeles, California. I still consider David Lifton to be a very good personal friend of mine. I was on *Hard Copy* for two consecutive days with other witnesses and assassination researchers. I also met Debra Conway of JFK Lancer, who for 12 years or more has encouraged me to tell my story and provided on more than one occasion an opportunity to do so.

In retrospect, I feel what I managed to do for Mrs. Kennedy and the remains of President Kennedy while in Parkland Memorial Hospital is what I hope anyone would have been proud and honored to do, given the same set of circumstances. I did what I felt had to be done; I did what I could. I was fully conscious of the situation that I was in, and acted sincerely, respectfully and as considerately as I possibly could, as did my dear friend Peanuts.

I am not the same daring young man who in 1963 raced daringly around the streets of Dallas with lights flashing and siren blaring. The ensuing years have added maturity, calmness and a more realistic view of life. I have had many years to reflect on what took place. As I consider my part in that historic day, I am satisfied that I did the best I could; because when important moments in life are thrust upon us, that is all anyone can do; that and stand later at the door of those memories.

A Tribute To Aubrey Rike

My Recollections of a Very Special Person

By David S. Lifton

A ubrey Rike is one of my favorite people. He's straightforward, honest, and has a wonderful sense of humor. Aubrey has lived a life of integrity. Indeed, that single word—"integrity"— stands out when I think of Aubrey Rike, what he has meant to me personally, and of the legacy he has left to history with regard to the Kennedy case.

If one goes back to the newspaper accounts from the weekend of President Kennedy's assassination, one finds the name "Aubrey Rike" mentioned as the person from the O'Neal funeral home who was at Parkland Hospital and who participated in placing the President's body into an expensive ceremonial casket. The casket was brought out to the hospital loading dock, and placed aboard the O'Neal ambulance. Then that ambulance, commandeered by Secret Service agents, brought President Kennedy's body from Parkland Hospital to Love Field, where that casket was placed aboard Air Force One.

Aubrey Rike played what at first appeared to be a minor role in the events of November 22, 1963. But as it turns out, his telling the truth about what he witnessed—and doing so in the most credible manner possible—has been important in arriving at certain larger truths about the JFK case. And that's what I admire most about Aubrey: he has not flinched at bearing truthful witness to what he personally saw. He has not taken a path of convenience. Rather, he has simply told the truth, permitted himself to be filmed (by me, in late October 1980), and then finally (and what was has been so valuable and impressive to me) Aubrey never changed his story. He neither embellished, nor elaborated. He simply told the same story again, and again, whenever the occasion arose.

So this is my tribute to Aubrey, and to explain why I feel this way, and admire him as I do, I must relate a small part of my own story, and explain how I first read about Aubrey in the press; then interviewed him over the telephone (in March, 1980) and then, finally, in October, 1980, came to his home in Plano, Texas (just outside Dallas) with a professional film crew, to record his story on camera.

* * *

Aubrey Rike's filmed account of what he witnessed at Parkland Hospital played a crucial role in permitting me to communicate certain fundamental truths about the JFK case to the public when *Best Evidence* was first released in January, 1981. Aubrey's filmed account was broadcast nationally, at the time, and many more times in the years following. Further, I can report from personal observation, made when showing the film at numerous colleges, and watching the reaction of college lecture audiences, that it is Aubrey Rike's very obviously truthful demeanor that has made all the difference. I hope my filmed interview of Aubrey will be available to future generations at the National Archives.

Now let me relate the story of how this all began.

* * *

We have all watched true-crime mysteries which dramatize a situation where arriving at the truth, and achieving justice, often depends on just one or two witnesses telling the unvarnished truth about what they saw. Considered in the abstract, telling the truth may seem like an easy thing to do, but it is not easy when that truth contradicts some "accepted" version of events for society at large.

The central thesis of my book, *Best Evidence*, is that the autopsy report was falsified, and in the following way. *Best Evidence* argues that President Kennedy's wounds were altered (and bullets removed from his body) between the time his body was first examined in the Emergency Room at Parkland Hospital (where he was pronounced dead) and the time of the autopsy that night, at Bethesda Naval Hospital. (By "altered," I am referring to both the removal of bullets from inside the body, and the altering of wounds on the surface of the body, so that, at autopsy, the body no longer provided an accurate "diagram" of the shooting; but rather was tantamount to a medical forgery).

I'll not belabor the point here with details of evidence concerning altered wounds. Suffice it to say that *Best Evidence* focuses on the President's body as evidence, stressing the obvious: that JFK's body—just as would be the case in any murder—was the most important evidence in the Dallas assassination. Further, that the President's wounds, competently interpreted (and assuming they were not tampered with) would provide the basis for establishing valid autopsy conclusions.

Finally, *Best Evidence* argues that if those wounds were altered prior to the autopsy performed some six hours later at Bethesda Naval Hospital outside Washington, D.C., then those autopsy conclusions—about the number and direction of the shots that struck the President (conclusions which in this case implicated Lee Oswald's rifle)—cannot be relied upon. Why? Because if the wounds were altered, then the autopsy conclusions about bullet trajectories would be invalid, because they were based on altered evidence. In short, the autopsy normally provides what is tantamount to a legal diagram of the shooting, but if the wounds have been altered, then the diagram is false.

This is where Aubrey Rike (and certain other witnesses) enter the picture, because obviously, the wounds could not have been altered unless the body was intercepted, and

Aubrey Rike's value as a witness stems from the crucial role his account plays in establishing the fact that the President's body did *not* make an uninterrupted journey from Dallas to Bethesda. In short, Aubrey Rike's account is important in establishing a break in the chain of possession of President Kennedy's body.

A law professor once explained it to me this way: if there is no valid chain of possession (or "chain of custody") of the President's body, then the Bethesda autopsy report is nothing more than a description of the way the President's body looked at 8 PM, the official "start time" for the Bethesda autopsy, but that does not necessarily bear any truthful relationship to the way it appeared, immediately after the shooting. Consequently, the wounds the body contained at Bethesda (if the wounds were altered) would not necessarily tell the true story of what happened in Dallas.

It is no secret that the Dallas doctors, based on the wounds they observed, thought the President was struck from the front—and only from the front. The Bethesda doctors came to exactly the opposite conclusion: that the President was shot twice, and only from behind.

Prior to the publication of *Best Evidence*, there were two commonly held positions with regard to the Warren Report and the medical evidence. Those defending the official version (i.e., the Warren Report) often took the position that the Dallas doctors were simply wrong; conversely, many of those who believed the Dallas doctors believed that the Bethesda doctors were simply liars. *Best Evidence* was the first book to argue that both groups of doctors were telling the truth, and that the body had been altered.

All of which highlights the importance of knowing whether or not the body arrived in Bethesda exactly in the same condition as when it left Dallas; and whether it made an uninterrupted journey between Dallas and Bethesda.

Aubrey Rike as a Key Witness
to a Covert Intercept

Part of the case that the President's body was altered (as presented in *Best Evidence*) is that it was covertly intercepted after it left Parkland Hospital and prior to its arrival at Bethesda some six hour later. Although that can be argued based on medical data about the wounds, it can also be inferred—and strongly so—from the evidence indicating there had been a covert intercept of the body, prior to its arrival at Bethesda. This becomes obvious when one compares the wrappings on the body (Dallas versus Bethesda) and the coffin used to transport the body (again, Dallas versus Bethesda). *Both* the wrappings on the body and the coffin containing the body had changed between Dallas and Bethesda.

Specifically: in Dallas, the President's body was wrapped in sheets and put into a regular full-sized ceremonial coffin; at Bethesda, the body arrived in a body bag, inside a shipping casket.

Aubrey Rike was a key witness in establishing that, in Dallas, President Kennedy's body had been wrapped in sheets—not a body bag—and that it had been placed in a full-sized ceremonial casket.

In writing *Best Evidence,* these facts were established on the basis of documents and interviews, and it was all laid out in the manuscript that was submitted to the publisher on April 1, 1980. But then came another challenge, the dimensions of which I had not entirely foreseen when I was writing the book: I would have to communicate this "before" and "after" situation, so seemingly easy to state in a manuscript, and in text form, in radio and TV appearances across the country, and on a national book tour arranged by my publisher.

Like most authors, I had conducted most of my interviews by telephone. Now I wondered how those telephone interviews would hold up, if subjected to skeptical media scrutiny. Would it be believable, based on my telephone interviews, augmented with certain documents, or would it have the quality of hard-to-believe and rather fantastic hearsay?

Some decades ago, Marshall McLuhan made the point that "the medium is the message." The fact is that, from press accounts, and from interviewing Aubrey on the phone, I knew very well what he had witnessed in Dallas—but in *Best Evidence*, that "message" was in text form. Now I worried that TV producers would smell an opportunity for a "story" and would want to meet the witnesses on whom I was relying, go over the same ground, again and again, on the telephone, and perhaps even send out a film crew, to interview them on camera.

It struck me that if I was going to do my job correctly, and effectively present the case I had written about in my book in a TV interview format, then I should have a filmed record of what Aubrey had told me, and some of the others, as well. I should interview Aubrey, myself, on camera, and have the film ready for viewing.

I interviewed Aubrey for the first time in March 1980, by telephone. When we spoke, I was struck with what a distressing experience November 22 had been for him, personally. Not only did he have very positive personal feelings towards the President and his wife, but it had been almost traumatizing for Aubrey to witness, at close hand, the brief but intense struggle between two law enforcement entities—the Secret Service, and the Dallas Police—in the struggle for possession of the body.

As to the basic concept of the intercept (and the fact that the body left Dallas wrapped in sheets, and in a ceremonial coffin, and yet at Bethesda was delivered in a body bag, which itself was inside a shipping casket) there were a number of witnesses at Bethesda who could establish these facts. One was Paul K. O'Connor, a Bethesda medical technician who was present when the body arrived in a shipping casket (which he helped open), and further, that the body was contained, inside that shipping casket, in a body bag (which he helped unzip).

The problem was how to make all this intelligible to the public, especially when it became apparent to me that news programs might want to contact Aubrey, contact the other witnesses (e.g., O'Connor) as well, and perhaps produce their own video documentary of my book. Furthermore, I wasn't sure what kind of interview they might conduct, how such film might be edited, and whether—after the process ran its course—the resultant filmed interviews would be in accordance with what the witnesses had told me, during my telephone interviews. Some ten years ago, I wrote a report on what happened next, how I decided to film the witnesses myself, and persuaded my book publisher to support that film project. Much of what follows is quoted directly from that report.

October 1980:
Putting the *Best Evidence* Witnesses on Film

As the weeks and months ticked by towards my scheduled January 1981 publication date, I realized there was an historic opportunity that would exist but once—right then—and that it would be very important to exploit it if at all possible.

The essential thesis of *Best Evidence* involved recognizing a "before" and "after" condition on President Kennedy's body: i.e., there were witnesses in Dallas who saw things one way (as regards the wounds), and witnesses at Bethesda who saw something entirely different. The same "before" and "after" situation applied to the wrappings on the body and the coffin used to ship the body from one location to the other.

I knew from telephone interviews that Aubrey Rike in Dallas had put the President's body in sheets, and helped lower the body into a large funeral casket, whereas when the body arrived at Bethesda, according to O'Connor, it was in a body bag inside a shipping casket. Rike wouldn't know until

Best Evidence was in the book stores that the way the body left Dallas was not the way in which it arrived at Bethesda.

Conversely, Paul O'Connor, at Bethesda, knew that the President had arrived in a body bag, but until *Best Evidence* was published, *he* would have no idea that that wasn't the way Kennedy's body left Dallas.

There could only be one "first time" to interview these critical witnesses, to capture the reaction of each of these witnesses when first exposed to this information which was so at variance with their own experiences. That time would have to be *before* the book was published, and I decided that I wanted to be there, to be the person doing these "first time" interviews, and to record their unvarnished, original reaction, on film. I wanted to be present and to preserve on film their astonishment, assuming that was the case, or whatever other reaction they might have.

So I proposed to Macmillan (my publisher) that we film about five of these witnesses. The situation: there were people at Bethesda who didn't know what the body looked like in Dallas; and those in Dallas who didn't know it was different at Bethesda. The same applied to the manner of transportation of the body—i.e., the wrappings on the body in Dallas, versus Bethesda; and the coffin used to transport the body—again, "Dallas versus Bethesda." Not that many witnesses would have to be filmed, to make the point. My goal was to capture both groups on camera, in their naive state; i.e., before they knew about the other, and then intercut the two in a short documentary film. I could then show excerpts from that film on my book tour, use it to brief news reporters, and later still show it to college lecture audiences. In short, my most critical witnesses—and Aubrey was one of them—would always be with me, in the form of a video cassette.

In 1980, there were no "digicams" or inexpensive miniature cameras for a consumer market. "Shooting a witness" on film meant hiring a professional film crew, and doing the shoot just as any TV news show might. That meant hiring a camera man, a soundman, perhaps a producer—and not only paying for those people, but paying for their transportation and lodging. Nonetheless, that's what I thought should be done, and my motive for doing this was chiefly historical. (There was no home video market to speak of in 1980, and U-Tube was 25 years away). In addition, excerpts from such a project could be used on talk shows and in public appearances when promoting *Best Evidence.*

My publisher saw the potential of such a project and gave the green light. I hired an experienced camera crew—producer/soundman Mark Dichter, and a cameraman, Dave Watts, people whose work regularly appeared on commercial TV. The project would be filmed on 16 mm color negative (there was no 8mm video format back then) and the production entailed all the equipment and cables required for a remote shoot.

In late October 1980, we left from JFK Airport with a five-city itinerary: in five days, we would go to Gainesville, Florida, for Paul O'Connor; San Antonio, Texas, for James Jenkins; Dallas, Texas, for Aubrey Rike; Hoopston, Illinois, for Dennis David, and Pittsburgh, Pennsylvania, for X-Ray technician Jerrol Custer.

I decided to purchase a body bag to show to the witnesses, on camera, and had carried it aboard the airplane. I wanted to show O'Connor the body bag, to get his affirmative reaction that yes, this is how Kennedy's body arrived at Bethesda; and Aubrey Rike, in Dallas, to get the opposite reaction—that no, he hadn't put Kennedy in a body bag in Dallas: that Kennedy's body had left just wrapped in sheets.

This is what I had been told in telephone interviews; now I wanted to record it on camera.

Key to the whole operation (and I was instructed to do this by a news editor who was also hired for the project): I would be challenging the witnesses about their most basic recollections, almost pretending I didn't believe them, to get their reaction—hopefully a strong reaction—on film. It was a risky strategy, because the book was already typeset, and it would have been very serious, if in October 1980, any of these witnesses reneged on their accounts.

We boarded a packed flight at JFK. As we were taking our seats, I remember wondering if, in all the hustle and bustle, we had brought the body bag. Turning around, I recall shouting over about ten rows of heads, "Mark, do you have the body bag?"

Heads turned, and in the post-9/11 world, with the Patriot Act, and air marshals on many flights, I don't want to conjecture as to what might have happened; but nothing did, and our plane took off.

In Gainesville, Florida, Paul O'Connor made clear that the body arrived in a body bag, inside a shipping casket. His reaction couldn't have been stronger. Two days later, I was in Plano, Texas, just outside of Dallas, and at the home of Aubrey Rike, and his lovely wife, Glenda. It was a nice sunny day, and we agreed that the filmed interview would take place outside.

Late October, 1980:
Interviewing Aubrey Rike on Camera

On November 22, Aubrey Rike---a man with movie star good looks---was the Dallas funeral attendant, working for the O'Neal funeral home, who was at Parkland Hospital and who helped put President Kennedy's body into the large, bronze, Dallas coffin. In October 1980, when I interviewed him in Dallas, he was a police sergeant with the Highland Park, Texas police. The interview was conducted outdoors, as we sat on chairs in his back yard.

Rike is a very straightforward and honest person. He appreciates understatement, which he will deliver with a twinkle in his eye. He also had a deep admiration for President Kennedy—and I will leave to Aubrey the telling of his own personal interaction with Jacqueline Kennedy, which illustrates his own caring, respectful, and humble nature.

From the standpoint of recording on film the concept that Kennedy's body had not made an uninterrupted journey from Dallas to Bethesda, Aubrey Rike was the "opposite bookend" to Paul O'Connor. Paul O'Connor (whom I had filmed just a day or two before) had attested to the fact that Kennedy's body was delivered to the morgue in a body bag, inside a shipping casket. Aubrey Rike was in Dallas; he was the "no body bag was used in Dallas" witness. The two were like matching bookends. In much the same manner in which, in my book, I had compared the Parkland Hospital observations (made in Dallas) to the Bethesda observations (made at the autopsy conducted at Bethesda Naval Hospital, outside Washington D.C.) with regard to the President's wounds, Aubrey Rike was the "before" to Paul O'Connor's "after" when it came to the wrappings on the body, and the coffin.

As unobtrusively as I could, I sat down for the interview with the green body bag in a carton between my legs. The camera started rolling, and Aubrey gave his account of the fancy nature of the Elgin Britannia coffin in which he had placed President Kennedy's body. Thinking ahead to when we would be editing the footage, I asked Aubrey a question about automobiles, one which I had already used on O'Connor: if one compared coffins to cars, was the Kennedy coffin a Volkswagon, or a Cadillac?

"A Cadillac" came the immediate response from Aubrey. (In Florida, just a day or two before, O'Connor had answered: "A Volkswagon.")

Then came the most serious part of Aubrey Rike's account—how he had personally taken the President's body, which was wrapped in sheets, and laid it in the coffin. And then the final moment: Closing the lid.

It was October, 1980—a full 17 years after the assassination—yet when Aubrey said "we closed the lid," he momentarily choked up, and for a moment I thought he might start to cry. Seventeen years after the President's murder, Aubrey's reaction was that strong; his memory, that intense.

I then had to do something almost inappropriate, but it had to be done to get Aubrey's response on camera: I had to challenge him. I had to challenge the basic reality that was so fundamental to his memories of November 22, 1963.

I told Aubrey that at Bethesda, I had interviewed witnesses who said the body arrived in a body bag. Aubrey looked incredulous—no, he said, the President's body had *not* been placed in a body bag. *Absolutely not.*

When I told him about Paul O'Connor's account of having received the body in a body bag, and how he (O'Connor) had to open it "from the top to the bottom and he had to unzip the zipper,"

Aubrey responded sharply (and shaking his head): "He didn't get one from us!"

Even though I knew I was risking my credibility, I persisted. I then asked Aubrey what surely must have appeared to him to have been an absolutely preposterous question: Whether it was possible he was mistaken, and that, contrary to his memory, was it nevertheless possible that he had in fact put President Kennedy's body inside a body bag? No, he replied, he had not. And by the look he gave me, I could tell he was wondering: *What in the world is this fellow driving at?* He repeatedly assured me they had not used a "crash bag"—Aubrey's term for a body bag. And now came the moment designed to get the strongest possible reaction from Aubrey, and capture it on film.

I unfurled the body bag, laid it out between us, tried to assure Aubrey that there was a reason for the questions I was asking, and proceeded to continue to challenge him on the issue. Was he sure, *absolutely sure*, the President's body had not been placed in a body bag? A body bag just like the one that was now stretched out between the two of us?

By his demeanor, it was obvious that Aubrey couldn't understand *why* I was pursuing this line of questioning, and his face showed the incredulity, even annoyance. I knew I was walking on thin ice. Instinctively, I liked Aubrey, and I knew he was a lovely person; but still, I had to press this line of questioning as far as I could, to get his reaction on camera. And so I did.

Finally, with camera film running out, but with the audio tape still recording his voice, Aubrey responded by going back to one of the most intensely personal aspects of his entire experience that day, to substantiate his repeated statements that of course no body bag had been used: "There couldn't have been a body bag," he said firmly but politely, because, *"I was the one who had the blood on my shirt and everything from the body. If he'd been in a crash bag, you couldn't have got any blood on you, [be]cause it's a sealed bag."* (emphasis added).

Aubrey's voice almost cracked when he made the statement—and he was close to tears. I knew this was sacred territory.

Indeed, at that moment, and when Aubrey made that simple statement, I had difficulty maintaining my own composure, but I wanted to appear professional, and managed to do so. In fact, when Aubrey spoke those startling and heartfelt words, the camera had just run out of film (and so the image of him speaking the last 12 words was not on the film) but the sound recorder was running just fine. So we had what is called "wild sound," an audio track (for that particular statement), but no video of Aubrey as he spoke the final twelve words.

Just days later, in a New York City editing room, Macmillan's publisher reviewed the footage and told me he did not want me to use that final quote (which included the piece of "wild sound")—he thought it was too emotional, and that incorporating it in the film would be "going too far." I could tell what he was thinking: "For God's sake, you're talking about the President's blood!" But Aubrey's honest and unvarnished words were *exactly* what I wanted. His obvious angst in the seconds preceding those words—especially when he said "we closed the lid" and then spoke about the

Aubrey Rike (top) and David Lifton (bottom), 1980 interview.
Photos Courtesy David Lifton, *Best Evidence* Documentary

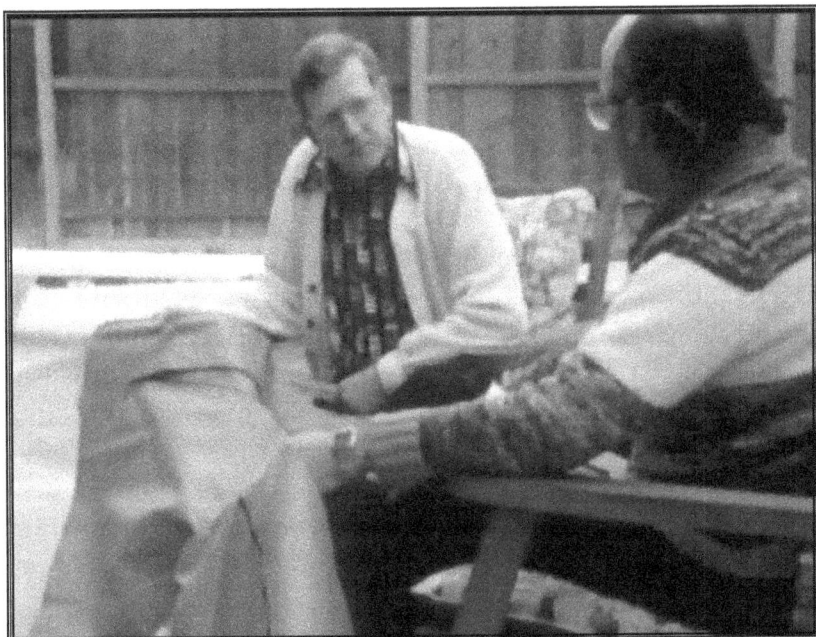

"No," he said, the President's body had *not* been placed in a body bag. "*Absolutely not.*"

blood on his own clothing—was so powerful, that I felt that piece of sound just had to be on the video. We argued about it intensely, right there at the editing console, the only real argument I ever had with my publisher. I prevailed, and the segment remained in the documentary (which became the *Best Evidence Video).*

Now what about the fact that the camera had just run out of film, at the moment Aubrey spoke those words? To maintain a film image on screen during those few brief seconds when Aubrey was speaking about the blood on his clothing (but when the camera had run out of film)—i.e., to "cover the shot," as film editors say, so the screen wouldn't "go to black"—we used a "reaction shot," a few seconds of me from another part of the interview, nodding at Aubrey as he spoke those emotionally charged words. In various college appearances, I have watched students reacting when the video is projected, and when Aubrey speaks those words, you can hear a pin drop.

I have always been proud that Aubrey's simple, yet powerful statement—his critical and most logical observation—is prominently included in a film that was shown to reporters, was broadcast nationally on a number of TV programs, and which ended up in a video that was distributed nationally, when the brief film was turned into a commercial video documentary in 1989.

* * *

After the Dallas interview, I left Aubrey's home, realizing that he very likely was wondering about my somewhat unorthodox line of questioning. Indeed, there were moments during the interview when I thought he might stop and say, "Who are you and why are you asking me these ridiculous questions?"

But it never came to that. When *Best Evidence* was published three months later, I made sure to send him a copy. Since then, we've been in contact a number of times. I know he understands why I brought a body bag to his home, produced it during the interview, and questioned him in the manner I did.

* * *

The interview I conducted with Aubrey Rike was replicated in the fall of 1988 by Stanhope Gould, the CBS producer who helped Walter Cronkite through the Watergate investgation. Stanhope, too, liked Aubrey. He confided to me, however, his own frustration. He said that despite his many years as a professional TV producer, and although he interviewed the very same witnesses I had, that his footage (filmed in 1988, and incorporated into a major TV documentary broadcast on San Francisco's KRON-TV and also on its sister station, in St. Louis) simply didn't compare to mine, filmed in 1980. He said that nothing could compare with the intensity and energy of the original interviews, filmed before any of the witnesses understood the full context of just what it was they were being questioned about. In particular, he cited my original interview with Aubrey Rike, and the incredulous look on Aubrey's face—indeed, his whole demeanor—as he answered the filmed challenges I had thrown his way, while a body bag lay unfurled between us.

> **David Lifton:** *And you didn't use a body bag for the President?*
> **Aubrey Rike:** *No sir, no way.*
>
> **David Lifton:** *Absolutely no question about that?*
> **Aubrey Rike:** *No way.*
>
> **David Lifton:** *How can you be certain?*
> **Aubrey Rike:** *I was there!*
>
> **David Lifton:** *And you remember?*

Aubrey Rike: *I remember picking him up. I was the one who had the blood on my shirt and everything from the body. If he'd been in a crash bag, you [couldn't have got any blood on you, 'cuz it's a sealed bag.] ((in brackets, no film))*

Stanhope said—and this was published in the San Francisco newspaper in the fall of 1988, at the time the documentary he had made was aired on KRON-TV in San Francisco—that the video I had made (contrasting Aubrey's account with that of Paul O'Connor, who received the body in a body bag)—constituted "courtroom quality evidence" that the President's body had been intercepted, and one of the reasons Stanhope made that statement, I am sure, came from the credibility that was so evident when Aubrey Rike appeared on camera.

Aftermath

I always wondered how the different witnesses I had filmed would react, after my book was published, and excerpts from the film were broadcast nationally. I never saw the *Best Evidence* witnesses as a "team" nor had I tried to recruit them as partisans of a theory. Their accounts were in the book; and, after October 1980, those accounts were on film—and the combination provided a faithful "snapshot" of what each witness had observed, exactly as told to me during telephone interviews in 1979-1980, and then on camera in October 1980. So my attitude was "Let the record speak," but I was always concerned about any witness whose account might change, over time, because I knew that opponents of my work would use any such "changes" as the basis to attack the credibility of the witness.

On this score, I have I have always admired Aubrey for his very restrained conduct. He was just so darn sober. He didn't let any fame go to his head. If the occasion arose to tell his story again, he told it, and it never deviated from the way he told it to me the first time. He didn't change details; he didn't elaborate. He didn't embellish. And I really appreciated that, because it spoke to his credibility.

Aubrey Rike and *60 Minutes*

Credibility was a key issue when I showed the *Best Evidence* footage to Don Hewitt, the Executive Producer of CBS-TV's *60 Minutes*, in December 1980. *60 Minutes* prided itself in doing investigative stories, and I was hoping that this nationally broadcast news magazine—number one in the ratings—would do a story about my book, which was then about four weeks prior to publication. I had every reason to be optimistic. Dan Rather—who later became the CBS anchor—was then one of the key "segment anchors" at *60 Minutes,* and in late November, Rather's producer, Steve Glauber, had visited our editing room. Glauber screened some of the footage (and particularly the Rike versus Paul O'Connor segments about the coffin change and the body bag) and was quite impressed. "Boy, Dan is going to love this!" he said. Indeed, it looked like the perfect story for *60 Minutes,* and it appeared that we had a real shot at airing these interviews on national TV, in conjunction with the publication of the book.

But it was not to be.

An appointment was made to screen the film at CBS headquarters for Don Hewitt, the Executive Producer, who would either say yea or nay to the project. Present, besides myself, were the top people from Macmillan—the publisher, the editor in chief, and one of their top lawyers. I sat quietly as the critical scenes, which I had watched so many times in the editing room, flashed by. I watched Rike tell his story, and the "Rike-versus-O'Connor" dichotomy develop, on screen. Sheets versus body bag; bronze ceremonial casket versus cheap shipping casket. The perfect story (or so it would seem)—just made for TV. When the lights went on, after a screening of about 40 minutes, Hewitt was amazed, but also very angry. He could see the witnesses weren't lying, but he simply could not accept what they were saying. And another factor (I thought), was in play: instead of *60 Minutes* going out, "finding a story," and then filming it (as was normally the case) here was an author who appeared before them, complete with the story *already* on film!

Did you pay these people?!, he screamed at me, right in front of Macmillan's publisher, the editor in chief, and their general counsel.

What a cheap shot, I thought.

"Yes," I replied, "A dollar for the release"—referring to the signed release one must ask each person to sign, before filming begins. In other words, Aubrey Rike (and Paul O'Connor, and the others) had each been paid a dollar, for telling the truth, to a camera.

After a while, Hewitt calmed down, and actually tried to arrange for *60 Minutes* to do a show, but one of their well known "segment anchors" would have to agree, and so private screenings were arranged for me to screen the film for Dan Rather, and Morley Safer. Neither would deal with it. After screening the footage, Rather (who was sitting next to me) tried to claim (with a perfectly straight face) that he simply couldn't understand why anyone would want to alter the President's body—since Oswald shot the President!

When I asked him how he explained the manifestly obvious difference between Aubrey Rike and Paul O'Connor on the question of the wrappings on the body, and the coffin, he said: "Well, perhaps you've found some witnesses who simply remember things a bit differently." (So much for the fact that both men were there.)

Morley Safer was far more thoughtful—he and I spent an hour, at least, alone in an editing room, reviewing the footage. He said he'd think about it. Some weeks later he left a message that he couldn't do a show on this—that it was simply not the kind of material that was appropriate for *60 Minutes*. At one meeting, Hewitt told me there couldn't have been a plot, because he knew RFK, and "Bobby would have told me." A year or two later, Don Hewitt was very angry when he learned that I had written that *60 Minutes* would only do stories where news could be "packaged as entertainment." Not so, he said, but he still wouldn't do a show on the topic, and so the first major filmed documentary on *Best Evidence* was done by Stanhope Gould, who interviewed Aubrey (as previously noted) and who had been at ABC's 20-20, but then moved on to KRON-TV in San Francisco.

But back to Aubrey.

I also appreciated the fact that fame did not cower him, or impress him. When Geraldo Rivera called him, to try to get him on his show, Aubrey related to me with some amusement what happened. For whatever reason, Aubrey just didn't care for Rivera (who happened to believe the official version), and so he declined to appear—and Rivera, apparently unaccustomed to rejection, was screaming at him on the phone: *"Do you realize who I am?! Do you realize who I am?!"*

Aubrey basically replied "Yes, I know who you are, and no, I don't want to be interviewed by you."

Aubrey Rike in Los Angeles—Circa 1990

Another rather colorful experience I had with Aubrey occurred when he and Paul O'Connor came to Los Angeles for a multi-part series about my work that was broadcast on *HARDCOPY*, a nationally syndicated show produced by Paramount TV. That show, and Aubrey's trip to Los Angeles, resulted from a good relationship I had with *HARDCOPY's* producer, Craig Haffner, and its Executive Producer, Peter Brennan.

I was always surprised that despite the fact that *Best Evidence* was a Book of the Month Club Selection, and despite its having spent 15 weeks on *The New Times* best-seller list, and despite all the detailed evidence that the wounds (both in the area of the head and neck) had been altered, there was still so much fundamental opposition to the basic idea of "body alteration." I don't think these psychological blocks bothered Aubrey all that much, because he had worked in a funeral home, and had been a police officer. He had encountered death in violent situations, and understood that the body was evidence.

But the reaction of many people was different: "Who could have planned to do this in advance?" and "How did it work. . ?" And questions that in effect started with : "Do you mean to tell me that. .."? etc.

Craig Haffner, one of the chief producer's for *HARDCOPY*, was another exception. Craig had an intense interest in history, and was more than happy to do several shows on the subject, dealing with the Kennedy assassination and *Best Evidence*, and in multiple segments. About five episodes were planned, and one of them dealt with the covert intercept of the body, and the fact that—from direct eyewitness testimony—it could be demonstrated that the body had left in sheets, and arrived in a body bag; and that it had left Dallas in an expensive ceremonial casket, and arrived in a cheap shipping casket. Aubrey Rike and Paul O'Connor being the chief witnesses who could attest to this state of affairs, on TV, both were flown out to California, and it was arranged they would meet in person, for the first time, on the show. During that trip, I took the opportunity to do my own separate re-interview of Aubrey, and Paul, which was quite detailed—in the living room of a friend. (That footage has never been used, but it is quite good).

At that time, the three of us—Aubrey, Paul, and I spent an afternoon just "hanging out." We ended up in my car, with some hours to spare, cruising around Hollywood, and Beverly

Hills. Like many people who were new to Los Angeles, they both wanted to see some of the sights.

I remember thinking: "Here I am, driving around with the guy that sent the President's body on its way, from Parkland Hospital in Dallas, wrapped in sheets, and the fellow that received it at Bethesda Naval Hospital that evening, in a body bag; and they're both in my car." It was as if I had "precious cargo" aboard.

At one point, we were in Beverly Hills, and driving on Sunset Boulevard, where "maps to the stars' homes" are sold. One of them, and it may have been Paul O'Connor, said he'd like to meet Paul Newman (or one of the major movie stars).

The other one (perhaps this was Aubrey) said "Well, they wouldn't want to meet *us!*"

And I said, "Don't be so sure. A lot of these Hollywood folks are *very* interested in the assassination" (and they are!) "They're real smart, and sometimes very political, and they don't know what happened in Dallas any more than anyone else, and they would love to spend an afternoon with two such important witnesses as you fellows." But unfortunately, that was not to pass, and we didn't knock on anyone's door.

Soon we ended up at the Santa Monica Pier, overlooking the Pacific Ocean, and in a lovely little restaurant there called "The Boat House," eating a very pleasant lunch, on a nice sunny day.

* * *

Almost 45 years have passed since 1963, and I believe that someday, we will in fact learn the full truth about the Kennedy assassination. Perhaps we will someday learn just who it was who contributed the bright idea that to control the autopsy, you didn't have to bribe the autopsy doctors (afterwards), or control them in some nefarious fashion, beforehand. All that was necessary was to alter the basic evidence being examined: the President's body.

Aubrey Rike is a witness to an important part of history: his account is important in establishing that there was a break in what lawyers call "the chain of possession." Aubrey not only possessed certain facts from his own observations, but in addition, there are more personal aspects to his story, as when he interacted with Jacqueline Kennedy, who said something very nice and complimentary about him. I can only say that if all the witnesses had the rectitude (and plain decency) of Aubrey Rike, and the observational powers and the integrity of Aubrey Rike, this case would be further along today. We would have benefited from a higher level of reliable data, and probably be closer to the truth. In any event, thank God for the Aubrey Rike's of the world.

I think so highly of him, I'm so pleased that I met him, and I'm grateful that I had the opportunity to film him. I'm sure that in the years to come, history will have kind things to say about Aubrey Rike, and I am honored to have been of service to Cleo, the Muse of History, and to have recorded Aubrey's critical account on film, and thus help to bring to future generations an important building block of the truth about the Kennedy assassination.

* * *

David S. Lifton
Los Angeles, California
9/27/08

Afterword

Colin McSween

I will always recall first meeting Aubrey Rike seventeen years ago in downtown Dallas. At the time, he was standing at the very location where he and Peanuts had collected an apparent epileptic seizure patient on Friday, November 22, 1963. He related to me a small portion of his involvement with the Kennedys on that fateful day in Dallas with amazing humility. He spoke as though he was simply retelling what his domestic errands had been on any given day. The more he talked, the more I quickly realized that this was the man whom I'd seen briefly in the 1964 David L. Wolper *Four Days In November* documentary, and David S. Lifton's book and research video *Best Evidence*. I then asked Aubrey if he had ever set about organizing a written account of that day in 1963, or any aspect of his recollections. That was, I suppose the first time that I personally ever suggested to him that he consider getting his story written.

Considering his role on that tragic day forty five years ago this fall of 2008, and the services that he and Peanuts had rendered, most people who had experienced such extraordinary circumstances might well be expected to have an attitude, airs, a swelled head or inflated sense of self importance. I was quite amazed by Aubrey's unaffecting manner and even more so by the genuine emotion displayed as he quietly shared with me his experiences and involvements on that dark, sad, November 1963 day in Dallas. We exchanged information about our respective professional lives and I suppose my being a licensed mortician with some experience in coroner's work and subsequently police departments helped Aubrey to relate to me and reveal more, perhaps, than what he may have otherwise done.

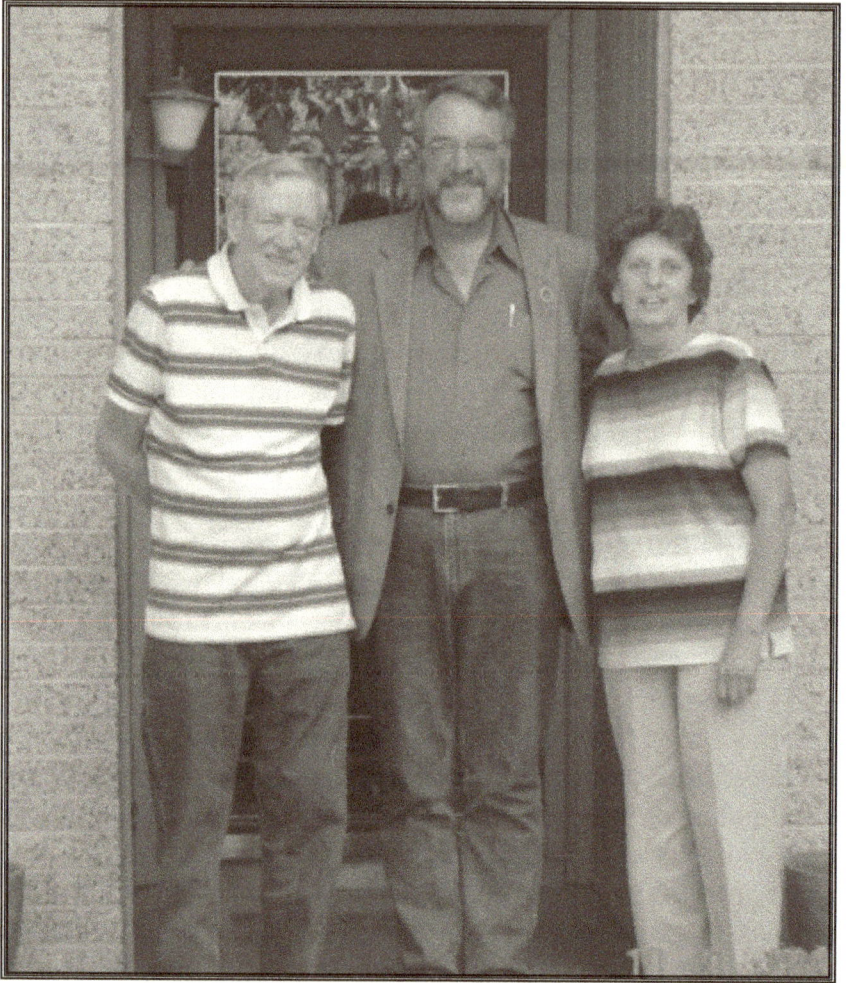

Left to Right; Aubrey, Colin & Glenda.
(D. Gurney & C. McSween, 2007)

I have always thought and felt that for me personally, in order to obtain a sense of connection and some reality, I've needed to be in the exact location where certain events took place, events that shook our world and shaped our history. I had been to Dallas and to Dealey Plaza ten years prior to this visit but being in Dealey Plaza with Aubrey Rike, in the exact location where he and Peanuts had collected their patient just seven or eight minutes before the assassination of President Kennedy, is quite unforgettable.

I remember asking him if he had ever been to Canada, in particular to my area. He said no, but he had been to Alaska by ship when he was with the Marines in the 1950s. So I asked him if he would ever consider coming up our way to visit, and maybe speak to a group, a Rotary club or other organization, concerning his experiences on November 22, 1963. He said he would like to very much and explained that his needs were quite simple. This of course, sat very well with my Scottish blood and we discussed the idea further, but I never actually managed to pull it off until the early 2000s with the help of some dear friends and colleagues of mine. On one such visit, we also managed to arrange to have Glenda along on the trip.

Over the many years following our first meeting in Dealey Plaza, Aubrey and I have managed a number of visits and outings together in which he has shown me the locations where many of his Dallas experiences unfolded, especially those of November 22, 1963. These visits were comprised of day and evening trips, and intensified as Aubrey and I engaged in getting his story into print. He still drives pretty fast too, even with his dear wife Glenda in the car with us. It is slower no doubt than his days at the wheel of ambulance #606, but plenty fast enough to indicate he was capable of fulfilling any schedule requirements during in his years driving an ambulance or as a police officer at the wheel of a police cruiser.

Aubrey is an honest, forthright, humble, giving public servant at heart. These characteristics are not simply adopted virtues assumed during the years he served in his various professions before retirement. Rather, they are an integral part of his character, and are what largely prompted him into vocations spent in the service of others.

Aubrey's character has been tested many times in his colorful and responsibility-laden life, but never like it was in Trauma Room 1 in Parkland Memorial Hospital that day in 1963. Considering what might and could have been the case, Aubrey was a genuine blessing and a gentleman to both President Kennedy and Mrs. Kennedy, and as such was addressed and acknowledged as such by Mrs. Kennedy in the presence of the Secret Service. I am fortunate that Aubrey saw me as a potential friend; one earnestly interested in his story, and in him as a person, and he therefore felt he could share with me his precious memories of that day of November 22, 1963.

Aubrey and his assistant Dennis McGuire, affectionately known as Peanuts, had the experience of waving at President Kennedy and the instant thrill of having the President return that wave right back at them just twelve minutes prior to the assassination. While Aubrey and Peanuts were technically still on the clock, they managed to get in on the excitement of watching a presidential motorcade and so far to date, the most famous presidential motorcade in history. Within a minute of this, their pleasant andpersonal exchange of greetings with the President, Aubrey and Peanuts were dispatched on yet another emergency ambulance call in the downtown area. This next ambulance call would providentially place them in the center and the thick of living history as it unfolded.

Aubrey and Peanuts took their patient to Parkland Memorial Hospital where the remnants of the president's motorcade would follow within mere minutes. Yet, although they were at the center of where the next sixty to ninety minutes of intense history would unfold, ironically they would not immediately hear the news of the shooting of the President.

As destiny would have it, Aubrey and Peanuts wound up as examples of those rare characters of chance who find themselves standing by in a quasi-official basis during some of the most unparalleled frightening, unsettling hours and minutes in the history of the United States and of the world. The President of the United States of America was dead, and the job they had to do was suddenly pitched into an event magnified to epic proportions.

These two very young men were summoned, impromptu, on an emergency basis at the demand of senior agents of the United States Secret Service while yet in the emergency corridors of Parkland Memorial Hospital immediately following the shooting of President Kennedy and Texas Governor John Connally. Aubrey and Peanuts were assigned to an unrehearsed, unscripted role that nothing could have ever suitably prepared them for and in response they fulfilled their roles with all of the emotional energy and depths of human compassion their souls could muster. Few people are at the ready to assume the type of unscripted, unplanned and unassigned role essential to providing selfless, heartfelt, unspeakable assistance.

In the 1991 movie *JFK*, a small portion of Aubrey and Peanuts' actions goes almost unnoticed, as the film recreates a small portion of the scene in which they collect the epileptic seizure patient off of the west side of North Houston Street. The scene was restaged and filmed on location where the original incident occurred. This footage is mixed amidst clips of original and restaged footage of the motorcade as it made its way through the city. Aubrey's story will no doubt also rekindle some level of interest in that movie.

Those recreated scenes of Peanuts' and Aubrey's ministrations to the Houston Street patient, were no doubt, well intended inclusion in the film. However, they are unfortunately crowded in with other footage and a voice-over narration unrelated to the ambulance scene that they are also unintentionally, yet effectively denied their rightful gravity upon the viewing audience.

Many people whom I have personally polled who have watched that film have seldom ever noticed the scene or understood where it tied in with the assassination story. Furthermore, the recreated scene of what is supposed to be the casketing of President Kennedy at Parkland Hospital falls far short of depicting what actually took place in those minutes in Trauma Room 1. For those who have now read Aubrey's account in this book will be in solid agreement. After all who else can tell this story but the man who was there?

The near manic conditions which pervaded the activities and the scene in which Aubrey and Peanuts found themselves in Parkland's Major Medicine that mid-day of Friday, November 22, 1963, both perplexed and amazed these accidental participants in the unfolding drama. These two men sat almost unnoticed atop a hospital cot observing mayhem and an almost lunatic display of arguing, cursing, fighting and blame making amongst the highest ranking officials of the day whom under any other circumstances would have behaved as "societies' best."

The experience was surreal, and the conduct of these people was pathetically tragic, and yet at the same time to Aubrey and Peanuts, it was also nothing short of amusing. Having to witness the unbecoming behaviors and goings on generated some awkward and uncomfortable moments as they attempted to stifle their own emotions as well as their burgeoning swells of a need to laugh at much of it. The idea that adults of such position could fight and accuse each other, much like a cluster of children might do over a broken vase, while at the same time remaining evidently numb to the tragedy that had placed them there, was a sad display of a lack of sensitivity and respect.

In the midst of the madness, however, were a number of constant, sobering, visual reminders of what was going on and why. Doctors, nurses and various specialists darted in and out of Trauma Room 1. Just 4 or 5 feet away and within easy listening distance of Aubrey and Peanuts, sat the lone, tragic figure of Jacqueline Kennedy dressed in her now famous strawberry pink, woolen suit with the deep, navy blue lapels. The situation in which these two ambulance attendants now found themselves was beyond belief, but the images, sights and sounds were not going to be simply wished or blinked away.

Without any rules in hand, a protocol manual to read, or any other formal instruction, Aubrey and Peanuts managed their way through a few short bits of conversation with the First Lady, politely restricting it to whatever she initiated. Their feelings ran deep for the First Lady and so did their sense of respect and propriety, unlike the conduct of those nearby, and within easy earshot, arguing dignitaries.

Aubrey's account of being asked by the Secret Service to obtain a casket for the President is even more sobering. This was the clearest indication at that moment in time that this was a once and forever irreversible event. Aubrey's recollection of entering Trauma Room 1 and seeing the deceased President lying on the emergency cart, his head enshrouded in a white sheet, is numbing. As a fellow practitioner of the funeral service profession I too, have been in death rooms in numerous settings to collect the remains of celebrities, but I am at a loss to imagine how I might have handled this same circumstance, or if I could have even maintained my physical equilibrium. With this added degree of insight, I can assure you that Aubrey and Peanuts handled the situation about as well as anyone in our profession would have wanted. He did us all proud!

To President Kennedy's fatally wounded physical presence on the treatment cart in Parkland's Trauma Room 1, Dr. Charles Crenshaw said, "Even in that condition, his charisma filled the room."

US Navy Medical Corpsman Paul O'Connor expressed about his own experience with the deceased President in the morgue at the US. Navy autopsy later that evening at Bethesda Naval Hospital, "He was dead, but he was the President of the United States and his physical presence and amazing aura filled the room. You could have heard a pin drop when we first laid eyes on him."

The experiences of the Catholic priests being summoned, witnessing the Last Rites being administered, Mrs. Kennedy placing her wedding ring on the finger of her dead husband, these are all painful and profoundly sad moments which to this day Aubrey cannot retell without his emotions resurfacing. He is, as they say in the film industry, "in the moment" but absolutely no acting is involved here. This is all genuine heart and soul and if someone had to be there to do the things that Aubrey did, then I for one am forever grateful that it was him.

Placing the President into the casket, closing the lid and sealing it had become by circumstance, rather than choice, part of Aubrey and Peanuts' duties that day. The verbal and physical battle between local Dallas County, Texas State and US Federal authorities over matters of legal jurisdiction in a homicide and the legal custody of the body was part of what Aubrey and Peanuts also witnessed.

The placement of the casketed remains of the President into the hearse, seating Mrs. Kennedy in the rear of the hearse, and the mad dash to Love Field Airport, was in many ways easier than anything else that Aubrey had had witnessed or participated in that day; but it also brought about some of his own first realizations of the tremendous depth of compassion and affection he had held for President and Mrs. Kennedy. Most of what had gone on since the noon hour was beyond belief, and at rare moments it seemed to Aubrey as though he would wake up at any moment to find it had all been a bad dream. However, a glance at his forearm and wrist would reveal the President's drying blood on his shirt sleeve and wrist watch and eliminated any such chance of it being simply a bad dream.

For Aubrey, seeing the casket disappear into Air force One was on some level an opportunity to attend a graveside service and a chance to say goodbye to a President he had held such deep admiration for, and whom had waved to him personally less than two hours earlier. Tears began to fill the eyes of one of Dallas' most strategically placed characters, one who also possessed one of its' greatest hearts. This became all the more evident as the presidential jet made its' way down the runway and then skyward as it departed Love Field Airport for Andrews Air Force Base.

A neurological dam of sorts had been holding Aubrey's emotions in check throughout the passing of the tragic events. Encounters with members of the press, requests for interviews, these events all continued to buffer or anesthetize the edges of nerves that were being slowly being frayed away, but Aubrey's day was far from over. Mercifully, Aubrey would later find himself a quiet, private place where an emotionally hellish dam broke loose for him, and at long last his feelings found some outward expression and release.

To anyone who has ever had the pleasure of knowing Aubrey Rike, he is a straight up guy, a true gentleman in every sense of the word. He is self-abasing, humble and astonishingly quite shy by nature. He has often expressed surprise that other people find his story worth hearing. In preparation for one of his visits to my home in western Canada to speak at a public forum on the assassination, as we discussed his travel plans, he asked one of our event organizers, "Do you mean to tell me that there are still people out there that really want to hear this old guy talk?"

Aubrey once suggested to me that I could do a fine job telling his story for him. "But," I said, "people need to hear it from your own mouth and in your own words." It is discussions such as these that helped prompt Aubrey's decision to get his story into print for historical purposes because as I said to him a number of times, one day neither he nor I will be here to tell it.

On one of my visits to Texas, Aubrey and I stopped for gas at a self-serve station just blocks from his home. It happened to be a November 22nd. He filled his gas tank and walked to the cashier's window to stand in line to pay. I watched him with wonder from the comfort of his car as a local Dallas radio station replayed some archival news coverage of the events of the assassination as originally aired on November 22, 1963.

Part of the replay featured the calm, reassuring voice of Mr. Bob Huffaker of WFAA TV who had been stationed during the immediate aftermath of the shooting outside the emergency entrance of Parkland Hospital. I wondered to myself whether anyone standing near or around Aubrey at that gas station had any idea whatsoever as to who Aubrey was, what he had witnessed, or what he had done on that day over forty years prior.

Aubrey returned to the car, and as we drove onto the freeway I told him what I had been listening to and what my thoughts had been. I asked him the same question I had considered—what people standing around might think about him. Without hesitation Aubrey said, "They probably think I'm just some old geezer, and they'd be about right, I guess."

That same evening one of the major news networks was boasting that they had a retired police officer that had been posted outside of the hospital emergency entrance on Friday, November 22, 1963. They went to great lengths to feature a live interview with this man on their evening news. Once this man was on the air, he had little to say of significance. He had seen little or nothing, not even the arrival of the President's car or motorcade remnants at the hospital, or the departure from the hospital, yet this man's information was somehow big news for a national news service. For the benefit of those wanting to know something of what was going on at the time on the inside of the hospital, this book may well be the last chance for readers to obtain a sensitive, inside account of what went on inside Major Medicine at Parkland Memorial Hospital from one who was there.

Many glimpses of the assassination shared by others are scholarly yet void of the emotionally raw and direct personal touches this book imparts. This book is therefore, somewhat of a rarity when relating details that few could have observed, unless they had been at the elbow of Aubrey Rike that day in 1963.

Aubrey's story is real, true, poignant history and needs telling over, and over, and over again; if for no other purpose than for the benefit of those who were not yet alive in 1963. It is for all generations that lived during the assassination, and for those yet to follow, to experience a sense of the enormity of the crime perpetrated on the streets of Dallas, Texas, on Friday November 22, 1963. At the same time, this book is to give readers a sense of the tender human dynamics experienced at the loss of a most remarkable and uniquely gifted leader in the history of our people, and in those personal lives that that loss immediately and indelibly touched forever.

Throughout the long years since, Aubrey has maintained a remarkably quiet humility about the event. He saw his actions then, sees them now, as simply doing what he could, in a manner that he felt that all people, regardless of their station in life, should be treated.

In my personal experience with Aubrey, he has always practiced this same approach when providing accounts of his life experiences, and in particular when recounting those of the assassination of President Kennedy. Aubrey is a genuine patriot and deeply respects the Office of President of the United States.

I cannot say for certain how many times I may have urged him to write his book. The first time I mentioned it was when we had our first curbside conversation in Dealey Plaza, 17 years ago. However, I have always felt he was the one who had to tell the story. He had many apprehensions about launching into the effort, but whenever we would be on the phone together, when he was in Canada with me or I was in Texas with him, our discussion would inevitably get back to the matter of writing or getting his account into some form of media that would tell his story, and which be there for the generations to follow.

When sending him photos of caskets in order to obtain one that he felt accurately resembled the Elgin Britannia, he would ask, "Are people really interested in this stuff? Why do they ask? Why do they want to know about all of this?"

His private nature and generally reserved manner is further reflected in his humility expressed so often when he would say, "I don't want to be blowing my own horn." Or "Do you really think people will want to read this stuff?"

But I know, whenever I've had opportunity to share Aubrey's story with people I've met, whether at one of my own presentations on the assassination or while on a flight at several thousand feet in the air, the information is met with rapt attention and profound reactions. In each circumstance, I wished Aubrey had been there to tell the story himself. With this account of his own recollections, the story is available for everyone to read, for themselves, for as long and as often as they may feel the need to. As one becomes acquainted with the role that Aubrey Lee Rike, fulfilled on that dark day in 1963, I am positive everyone will deem this account an absolute must read.

At a point in the early 2000s, at a mutual decision, I sent Aubrey a package providing him with what I called trigger notes, an outline of sorts to serve as a framework on which he could structure his story. After numerous emails, snail mails, long distance telephone calls and personal visits, the idea evidently took hold. When Aubrey and Glenda came to Canada together in September 2006, I met them at the Vancouver Airport along with some close, dear friends of mine, Bruce and Jenny Clark. I embraced Glenda and Aubrey and as I did so, he slipped something into my shirt pocket, which I was almost ashamed to look at because I though it might be money or some such unwarranted token. When I retrieved the item I discovered it was an audiotape.

Aubrey immediately said, "That's my story, buddy. Get busy writing."

For me, obtaining the bulk of information out of him for this book has proven to be nothing short of herculean at times. Aubrey is humble, and essentially a man of few words, very few words. I recall sitting in his dimly lit office with him, both of us at the computer terminal in his home late one night, both of us growing punchy from a long day.

This book is about as much of his story Aubrey is willing to share in print, at least for now. I know of many more stories of his daring ambulance escapades, military career, and frightening police calls. He is my friend, and as such, has shared his life freely as friends often do.

I am personally eternally grateful to Aubrey and Glenda for deciding, among all the available talent out there, to trust and allow me this amazing privilege to assist them in getting their story into print. I thank my dear wife, Pat, for allowing me the time, endless hours and expense involved in the entire process.

As I have said to Aubrey many times now "Thank you, Aubrey for sharing and for giving of yourself." And as I have said to Glenda, "Thank you, Glenda, for being willing to share your husband in this way." I also thank the Almighty for having placed this couple so strategically where and when He did. I am thankful for their generous and gracious character, and their most unique role in making a horrible experience, in so many ways, just a bit more tolerable for Jacqueline Kennedy.

Colin McSween
October 2008

Appendices

Appendix 1

Background Notes

The following notes are offered by Colin McSween for the reader who wishes additional historical or background information.

Chapter 6: Page 25
Some people may find this hard to believe, but for whatever reason I was quite unaware that President Kennedy was going to be in Dallas that day...

Some managed to secure vantage points either at Love Field Airport or along the motorcade route. For those of the more privileged elite – they already had a place reserved for them at the $1000 per plate steak luncheon scheduled for 1:00 PM at the new Dallas Trade Mart on Stemmons Freeway.

It had rained through much of the night of November 21st and into the morning of the 22nd until about 9:00 AM. By 11:00 AM the weather couldn't have been better. The sun rose high against a brilliant blue, almost cloudless sky while the wind settled into a twenty mile per hour breeze and the temperature had risen to a pleasant 68 degrees. The crowds already lining the airport fence and the motorcade route were the apparent beneficiaries of what was looking to be a perfect day.

At approximately 10:30 or 11:00 AM, [Aubrey and Peanuts] were dispatched to yet another emergency ambulance call...

During the span of time in which Aubrey and Peanuts were engaged on this ambulance call, Air Force One had departed Carswell Air Force Base in Fort Worth and made the short fifteen minute trip to Dallas' Love Field Airport. The trip was so short that the Boeing 707 VC-137C had barely reached an altitude of five thousand feet before beginning its descent to the city of Dallas.

Air Force One, the presidential jet, touched down at Love Field at 11:38 AM and taxied to a stop at Gate 28 of the East Concourse of Love Field Airport. There the Kennedy's deplaned to an enthusiastic welcome from a large cheering crowd that was penned behind a cyclone fence, quite beyond reaching the President and First Lady unless the First Couple were to approach them.

After making their way through the official greeting line of local and state dignitaries, President and Mrs. Kennedy broke with normal protocol, walked over to the cyclone fence, and graciously greeted as many of the crowd as time would permit. This additional time taken with the crowd had delayed the start of the motorcade and would therefore also make them fall somewhat behind schedule.

The Kennedy's shook hands and exchanged verbal pleasantries with many of the citizens who had so anxiously awaited their arrival. This was a definite bonus for those who had braved the wind and earlier rain. Seventeen minutes passed since Air Force One had landed before President and Mrs. Kennedy were seated in the presidential limousine and the motorcade began to roll. They drove out Aviation Drive to Cedar Springs before heading out of the airport property and then east on Mockingbird Lane and past the Coca Cola bottling plant where they turned right onto Lemmon Avenue.

By 12 PM, the motorcade was traveling south on Lemmon and the lead cars were about to pass beneath the Continental overpass at Lomo Alto, at approximately the same time Aubrey and Peanuts cleared from their latest ambulance trip at Baylor Hospital, which was 12:05PM.

Among the many streets the motorcade crossed while on Lemmon was Reagan Street. "Father Oscar Huber of nearby Holy Trinity Catholic Church was standing on the east side of the intersection of Lemmon and Reagan where he managed to exchenge waves with the President as the limousine drove by. Within the hour, Father Huber would administer the Last

Rites of the Roman Catholic Church to President Kennedy in Parkland Hospital's Trauma Room 1.

After passing Reagan Street, the motorcade crossed Oak Lawn Avenue at 12:11PM and was at that point within a block and a half of O'Neal Funeral Home. From Oak Lawn Avenue, it proceeded down a gentle incline running alongside of Robert E. Lee Park before turning right onto Turtle Creek Boulevard, through Robert E. Lee Park before rejoining Cedar Springs Road. From there it traveled south-west to the intersection of Cedar Springs and Harwood where Aubrey and Peanuts would exchange waves with President Kennedy.

Chapter 7: Page 29
When we got to the location, we found a man lying on the sidewalk on the west side of Houston Street...

This location was within 100 feet or so of the south entrance of the Texas School Book Depository Building more or less directly in line with the front of the main public entrance to the Depository Building. This particular section of Houston Street was also a prominent, key roadway for the presidential motorcade route.

Chapter 7: Page 30
At the time, the man did not appear to me to have suffered an epileptic seizure...

It should be noted for historians and researchers that so far as Aubrey Rike is concerned the epileptic seizure incident, accounted for in Chapter 7, was probably a genuine coincidence. As far as Aubrey is concerned, the FBI's investigation that was later documented in the spring of 1964 satisfactorily addressed and answered the questions pertaining to the event.

Aubrey says, however, "Looking back at the days leading up to President Kennedy's visit to Dallas, I remember that we had been receiving what would ultimately be categorized as bogus emergency ambulance calls through our switchboard at O'Neal's. When you get a call you have to assume that it is legitimate. Occassionally, our dispatcher would send us out on calls in our ambulances, and upon arrival we would find there was no one there and apparently no substance to the call. These locations were at various places around the downtown area. It has been suggested we were being timed on how long it was taking us to get to these various places."

"The way in which the man seemed to almost vanish from the emergency department within the half hour that we'd placed him in the stall in Major Medicine at Radiology," is another point that Aubrey has often wondered about. Aubrey doesn't know if they did anything further with him in the way of examination or treatment of any kind there at Parkland. Aubrey just knows that the desk in Major Medicine where he placed the phone call to Mr. O'Neal to bring a casket, was immediately adjacent to stall number eight where he had placed the epileptic. "When I was there using the phone I noticed that he was gone."

But certainly, the epileptic seizure event, genuine or not, generated significant interest with the Dallas Police as it was addressed with some excitement on their two-way radio on channel 2 at 12:48 PM, 17 minutes after the assassination in Dealey Plaza. (See appendix 3 in this book entitled "Police Communications & Time Line.")

The matter was also of interest to the FBI as they also investigated the matter to the satisfaction of many, including Aubrey. Two separate documents were filed by the FBI on the incident. One is dated May 28, 1964 and the other is dated June 11, 1964. Copies of these two FBI reports and a transcript of the Dallas Police alert of November 22, 1963 are included in this book.

Chapter 7: Page 30

I took a different route to Parkland Memorial Hospital than the one the driver of the President's limousine would take...

During the brief few minutes that passed while Aubrey and Peanuts ran their patient to Parkland Hospital using lights and siren, the presidential motorcade had continued south on Harwood Street to Main Street where it then turned due west on Houston Street all the way to Houston Street at Dealey Plaza. As the motorcade wound its way through Dealey Plaza, the leading cars including the presidential limousine had entered the 400 block of Elm Street and had passed the Texas School Book Depository Building.

At mere seconds after 12:30 PM gunshots exploded over the cheers of the unsuspecting crowds. Suddenly what had been a seemingly well-conducted and an evidently enthusiastically received event became one of absolute shock and unbelievable horror. Both the President of the United States and the Governor of the State of Texas lay grievously wounded in the rear of the presidential car.

In the lead car immediately ahead of the President's car, Dallas Police Chief Jesse Curry immediately radioed the dispatcher and all escorting officers to get them to Parkland Hospital. Chief Curry also called for his other men to move to the railroad overpass and railroad right-of-way, to "Hold everything secure until homicide and other investigators should get there." He then added, "Looks like the President has been hit. Have Parkland stand by." The dispatcher replied, "Parkland has been notified. 12:32."

The presidential car had initially pulled out of line from the center lane on Elm Street to the right hand lane at which time it had sped off underneath the railroad underpass and ahead of Chief Curry's car. Upon reaching the on ramp to the Stemmons Freeway the presidential car had come to a temporary stop (beneath the vantage point of Ed Hoffman) in order to allow Chief Curry to once again take the lead before they continued northbound onto Stemmons Freeway and to Parkland Hospital.

On Stemmons Freeway the presidential limousines' newly rebuilt high performance 430 cid Windsor V-8 engine with its four-barreled carburetor was hurtling the four ton car along the freeway at speeds of 70 to 100 miles per hour. Secret Service agent Clinton Hill was doing all that he could just to hang on to the car, while using his body as a shield to provide some physical cover for the passengers from whatever else might befall them.

Upon receiving word from the Dallas Police radio room of the shooting, the hospital emergency room had given a *stat* call over the PA system sent out to alert Dr. Shires. The *stat* call immediately caught the attention of other emergency physicians who knew that Dr. Shires was away speaking at a medical conference in Houston, Texas that same day.

It is most likely that the *stat* call and initial alert to the physicians took place while Aubrey and Peanuts had been unloading their patient and wheeling him to the front desk of the emergency department. Procedures were already underway in both Minor and Major Medicine to clear those areas, but these areas were not visible from the emergency departments' front entrance. By the time that Aubrey and Peanuts arrived inside the emergency department front desk, much of this activity was underway, but it was not visibly evident to them.

Within seconds of the presidential car having come to a complete stop alongside of Aubrey's ambulance in the hospital's emergency ambulance dock, Secret Service agent Clinton Hill had removed his suit coat and placed it over the stricken President's head and upper torso almost as a partial shroud or as a pall.

During the flight of the presidential limousine along Stemmons Freeway, Jackie Kennedy had removed her strawberry pink suit's matching pillbox hat. It had become loosened in the wind generated by the high rate of speed of the limousine and been bobbing about on her head. The hat, being held on by only one or two hat pins, had been removed by the First Lady herself.

Chapter 8: Page 35
While we were redressing the gurney, President Kennedy had been placed in Trauma Room 1…

Emergency medical procedures had been initiated at about 12:43PM in Trauma Room 1 by the emergency physicians in an all out effort to maintain the President's remaining vital signs. Jacqueline Kennedy had entered the room a few times to see what she could. On one of these visits to the trauma room she had offered to Dr. Marion "Pepper" Jenkins some of the remnants of her husband's scalp and brain that she had managed to scoop off of the rear trunk deck of the limousine while the car while still in Dealey Plaza in the mad seconds immediately after the shooting.

Dr. Philip Earl Williams, had located and brought a brown metal folding chair for the First Lady to sit on while she sat waiting through her ordeal. During a visit between myself and Dr. Williams in his Dallas area office on November 23, 2004, he said, "I just did what I could, as little as it may have been. When you can't change events that have already occurred you just do what you can to make things as bearable or as comfortable as possible. It is hard to really imagine what that poor woman must have seen when her husband was shot."

Everything that could be done for President Kennedy was being done as fast as humanly and medically possible. As Dr. Paul Peters said in an interview some 35 years later, "We did what I would consider to be a commendable job in our efforts to save the President's life, given the equipment that we had, even by today's standards."

Chapter 10: Page 46
We noticed that fluids had already begun to settle into the tissues of his back as a result of gravity...

The blood that Aubrey refers to in this context had undergone a natural after death or post mortem change; the gravitational settling of the remaining blood volume into the deeper and more dependant posterior tissues of the body. The blood, being no longer circulated by a living cardiovascular system, is now subject to all the gravitational, chemical, microbiological and other environmental forces of nature. Being no longer circulated by a beating heart it has been left to settle by gravity to the lower areas of the body. Alternate terms used to describe or to define this after death phenomena include: Suggilation, Hypostasis, Lividity, Livor Mortis, Laking and even Pooling.

Furthermore, this hypostatic blood, no longer being re-oxygenated by the lungs it now no longer appears to be red ion color. Instead, the blood gradually becomes characteristically dark, blue to purple, and finally to an almost blackened shade that is observed in the host tissues where it settles.

Chapter 10: Page 46
In this particular case we were asked to simply ensure the basic and immediate sanitary needs of the body...

As frustrating as this may seem for researchers now or for others interested in the medical or forensic aspects of the case who wish for more information, Aubrey and Peanuts were neither assigned to nor were they trained to do any forensic work or to make any determinations of a medical or ballistic nature.

Aubrey did have prior experience performing embalming duties for his employer Mr. Vernon B. O'Neal and he could well have performed those same duties on the remains of President Kennedy had such been requested by Mrs. Kennedy or by the federal authorities. However, such were not his orders in this particular instance.

Had embalming been a task that Aubrey had been assigned to perform, he would then have been much more aware of the wounds inflicted on the President's body as the process of arterial injection would have made any areas of invasive trauma quite noticeable. In addition, the closure and sealing of any wounds is of paramount responsibility to a mortician/embalmer. At the very least, the body would have been entirely disrobed and the head in its totality would have had to be exposed in order for the embalmer to have been able to perform his work. However, as it was Aubrey said, "I never did actually see the forehead for myself, nor did I see the actual head or skull wound."

In most cases of a repatriation (shipping a body by public carrier, either by road rail, or air to another county, state, country, etc.) of a dead human body, it is customary, and in most instances a legal requirement, that the dead human body be embalmed prior to being placed aboard a public carrier.

However, Air Force One while being a passenger jet, was not deemed a public carrier per se' but was in actual fact the property of the United States Air Force and therefore embalming was not a legal requirement, but was a matter of discretion that could have been decided on by federal authorities. Furthermore, it is unusual to have embalming performed prior to an autopsy being conducted. Theran Ward's Certification of Vital Record or Certification of Death on President Kennedy indicated that an Autopsy "Was Held," however, no autopsy was held in Dallas County at all.

Chapter 10: Page 46
It was not painful, but I could feel the jagged edges of the bones through the sheet...

Aubrey's description of the fatal head/skull wound squares up with unimpeachable agreement and clarity with the hand drawn illustration of the same head wound of President Kennedy that Dr. Robert McLelland had drawn in 1966 for Josiah Thompson's book *Six Seconds In Dallas*.

Chapter 10: Page 49
It was a solid bronze casket and weighed about 400 pounds when empty...

The casket that the O'Neal Funeral Home provided for the repatriation of President Kennedy back to Washington, DC was marketed under the name the Elgin Britannia. It had formed oval urna corners and what is known as a swell-top or oval panel lid.

The Elgin Britannia casket was fitted with full length bar handles or extension bar handles along both sides of the casket that ran the length of the casket that pivoted outward in order to accommodate pallbearer's hands while being lifted or carried. The exterior was finished in a rich, deep, dark brown shade (or an oxidized patina) that imparted an appearance similar to an exotic wood tone that had a glazed, polished finish added to the surface.

Many such finishes when applied to metal and semi-precious metal caskets such as copper or bronze have the effect of making the item look to some people to be plastic under certain lighting conditions. Such was the case with Parkland Hospital's Neurosurgery Department Chief Dr. Kemp Clark. In his statement that he completed that same afternoon, he noted that President Kennedy had been, ."..taken out of the hospital in a bronze colored plastic casket..."

The quality of the casket at the time was such that even without a full service being provided by a mortuary, the casket on its' own would have easily cost between $2000 and $2500 in 1963. A new full-sized 1963 or 1964 Pontiac Sedan could be purchased at that time for about the same price. For the era, it was hard to imagine getting anything better than the Elgin

Britannia. It is little wonder why Aubrey and Mr. O'Neal both assumed that the President would be buried in the casket.

Additional data is further explored pertaining to the Elgin Britannia or the Dallas casket in a subsequent appendix entitled "The Dallas Casket & The Shipping Casket."

Chapter 11: Page 51
Father Huber was compassionately attentive to Mrs. Kennedy…

The Priest who performed this sacrament was the Very Reverend Oscar L. Huber. Father Huber has stated in interviews that although President Kennedy appeared to be dead, his soul may have still been within his body, and therefore the President could have accepted the sacrament before his soul left his body.

The following text is taken from *Time* Magazine dated Friday, November 29, 1963.

At 12:45, two Roman Catholic priests went swiftly into the emergency room. A policeman came out. "How is he?" a reporter asked. "He's dead," came the reply. Assistant Press Secretary Malcolm Kilduff appeared. To a deluge of questions, he screamed, "I can't say, I just can't say!" Last Rites. But he was dead. It was about 1 p.m. The Very Rev. Oscar L. Huber drew back a sheet that covered the President's face, and anointed John Kennedy's forehead with oil. He gave him conditional absolution—tendered when a priest has no way of knowing the victim's mind or whether the soul has yet left the body.

In Latin, Father Huber said, "I absolve you from all censures and sins in the name of the Father, and of the Son and of the Holy Spirit. Amen. If you are living, may the Lord by this holy anointing forgive whatever you have sinned. Amen. I, by the faculty given to me by the Apostolic See, grant to you a plenary indulgence and remission of all sins and I bless you. In the name of the Father and of the Son and of the Holy Spirit. Amen."

Then he covered the President's face once more with the sheet and in English offered the prayers for the Dying and for the Departed Soul:

"May the most clement Virgin Mary, Mother of God, the most loving consoler of the afflicted, commend to her Son the soul of this servant, John . . . Jesus, Mary and Joseph, assist me in my last agony. Jesus, Mary and Joseph, may I sleep and rest in peace in your holy company . . . Grant, O Lord, that while we here lament the departure of Your servant, we may ever remember that we are most certainly to follow him. Give us grace to prepare for that last hour by a good life, that we may not be surprised by a sudden death but be ever watching, for when Thou shall call that soul, we may enter eternal glory through Christ, Our Lord. Eternal rest grant him, O Lord and let perpetual light shine upon him. Amen." Jacqueline Kennedy stood next to the President's body, and with a clear voice, prayed with the others: "Our Father, Who art in Heaven . . ." and "Hail, Mary, full of grace. . . ."

End of quote from *Time* Magazine.

Chapter 11: Page 52
We closed the casket lid, sealed it and the priest placed a crucifix on top...

For persons who may be otherwise unaware, in the funeral profession there are as many different types of caskets as there are cars. One major significant difference among caskets is whether a casket is a Protective or a Non-Protective casket. A Protective casket is always either a metal casket or a semi-precious metal casket such as copper or bronze. These are fitted with a rubber gasket at any and all of the seams where the casket is capable of being opened. On account of the rubber gasket a protective casket can be sealed so as to make it air and watertight.

Non-Protective caskets do not seal air and water tight and although they may have various mechanical means of being secured in the closed position, maybe even locking, they do not actually seal in the true sense of the word. The Elgin Britannia casket that the O'Neal Funeral home provided for President Kennedy was a Protective casket and was equipped to seal air and watertight.

Chapter 11: Page 52
It has been reported by various writers and assassination researchers over the years...

According to presidential aide Lawrence (Larry) O'Brien, the casket handle was indeed damaged while the casket was being loaded onto the plane and passed through the rear left cabin door of Air Force One. As can be seen in the Cecil Stoughton photographs taken during the loading of the Dallas casket onto Air Force One, Mr. O'Brien had stood at the bottom of the passenger ramp/stairs with Mrs. Kennedy watching diligently as the bronze casket was carried up the stairs and passed through the cabin door. Mr. O'Brien repeated this account numerous times including during a television special commemorating the 25th anniversary of the assassination in 1988.

On a personal note, I have measured the width of the opening of the rear left passenger entry door of SAM 86970 where it is now in retirement at the Museum Of Flight in Seattle, Washington. It too, is a Boeing 707 jet aircraft & a former Air Force One. It has the exact same size door openings as was on SAM 26000, which was used as Air Force One in 1963. I have measured the opening of that jet's doorway and have compared it to the Solid Bronze Casket featured in this book's photographic section and can see just how easily that damage could have been sustained by a casket handle.

Chapter 11: Page 56
I jerked open the rear door of the hearse...

There are two principal body style options available in hearses, the landau style and the limousine style. The Landau type has a 60-70% enclosed rear casket compartment with decorative landau bars that are placed in visual reminiscence of the antique carriages once used many years before.

Mr. O'Neal's new hearse was the limousine style. In this instance, the casket compartment has an almost complete enclosure of glass or windows in place of solid metal wall panels. These vehicles were much more like a conventional station wagon of the 1950s and 1960s. These windowed panels gave the vehicle more of an ambulance look of the era and the more so if the vehicle were painted white such as Mr. O'Neal's new hearse.

In fact, this particular 1964 Cadillac was also a multipurpose car in that it could also be used as a transfer ambulance if need be. It was also equipped with a rear compartment folding attendant's seat which was to be occupied by Jacqueline Kennedy on the ride back out to Air Force One.

The resemblance of this vehicle to an ambulance was not lost on Dr. Kemp Clark, or the *Dallas Morning News*. Dr. Clark wrote in his Statement the afternoon of November 22, 1963 that President Kennedy had left the hospital ."..in an O'Neal ambulance. The *Dallas Morning News* had stated, "At approximately 2:05 p.m. the body was placed in a cream colored ambulance..."

Chapter 12: Page 59
We used an airport service road around to the east concourse that intersects with Aviation Drive...

Air Force Two (SAM 970 or SAM 86970) which had carried Vice President and Mrs. Johnson to Dallas that morning was still standing by at Love Field. Lyndon B. Johnson was now the 36th President of the United States by virtue of the United States Federal Constitutional ruling on the matter of Presidential Succession and he was already on board Air Force One (SAM 26000).

In order to make room in the rear of the passenger compartment of Air Force One for the Dallas casket, members of the crew of Air Force One and Air Force Two had removed a section of seats from the rear cabin area nearer the rear doors on SAM 26000 and had stowed them on SAM 86970.

Chapter 13: Page 63
Mr. O'Neal drove away in the hearse headed toward the funeral home…

It is understandable when an establishment such as O'Neal Funeral Home provides services on a death call (what is known in the funeral business as a "first call") to any extent that personnel, a casket, a hearse and any other physical services are rendered, that some recognition is in some circumstances merited.

Even though many other attendant duties may not have been required of the O'Neal firm, the first call as such was in most every respect a call that O'Neal Funeral Home had in fact serviced. Therefore, Mr. O'Neal saw fit to place an obituary notice in the local papers. The obituary notice that Mr. O'Neal placed and which is featured in this book, was published in the *Dallas Moring News* on Saturday, November 23, 1963.

However, if nothing else, it no doubt served as a small, inexpensive focus of the people's grief that sad weekend, a token of significant comfort and as a keepsake to be placed in photo albums, prayers books or bibles that very likely helped provide some sense of reality and closure in the matter for many people.

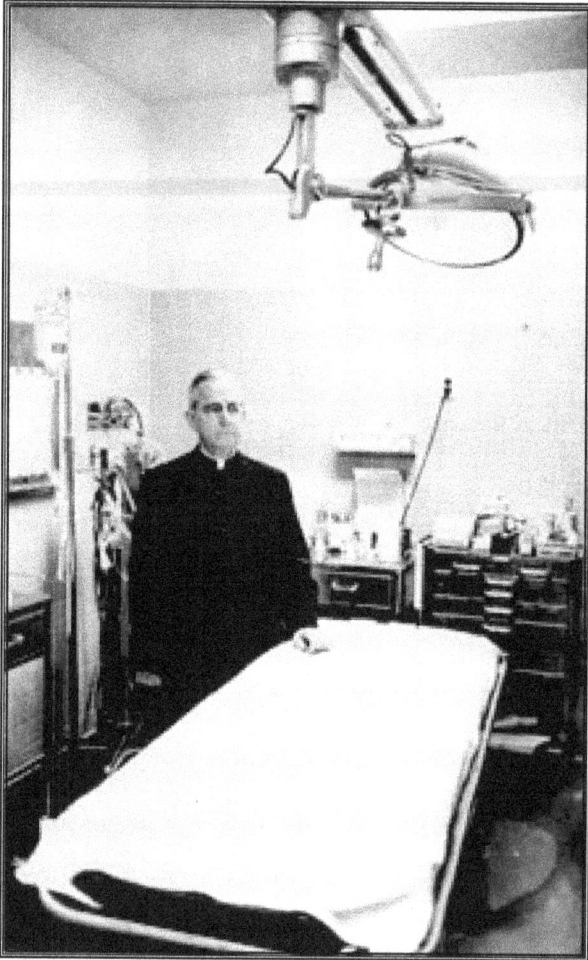

The Rev. Oscar Huber, pastor of Holy Trinity Catholic Church in Dallas, revisits the tiny Trauma Room No. 1 at Parkland Memorial Hospital one year after he administered last rites to dying President John F. Kennedy on November 22, 1963. The entire contents of the room are now stored in a National Archives facility in Lenexa, Kan., outside of Kansas City, Mo. (AP/File, 1964)

Bronze plaque identifying the interior area of the original site of Trauma Room 1 where President Kennedy was treated, expired and placed in the casket. (D. Gurney & C. McSween, 2007)

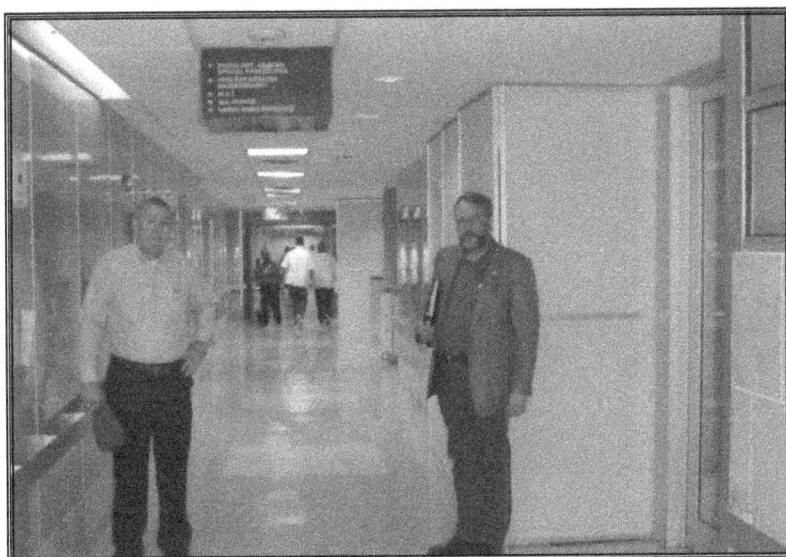

The original location of the trauma corridor in 1963. Chuck Wade (L) stands where Aubrey & Peanuts had sat on a hospital cot immediately outside Trauma Room 2. The Scrub & Linen Room was also on the left, just immediately beyond where Chuck is standing. Colin McSween (R) stands where Mrs. Kennedy had been seated immediately outside of Trauma Room 1. (D. Gurney & C. McSween, 2007)

Dudley M. Hughes Funeral Home at 400 East Jefferson Blvd. In Oak Cliff. This firm landed the City of Dallas ambulance service contract in 1961 & in turn subcontracted to Vernon B. O'Neal. On Monday November 25, 1963 Hughes provided the funeral services for Dallas Police Officer J.D. Tippitt. (D. Gurney & C. McSween, 2007)

3206 Oak Lawn, Dallas. Original location of O'Neal Funeral Home & Ambulance Service. The driveway between the existing buildings shown is where the original ambulance ramp was located. (D. Gurney & C. McSween, 2007)

Intersection of Cedar Springs Road & Harwood Street. It was at a
position near the south-east corner (shown across this intersection)
where Aubrey & Peanuts parked behind the crowd & watched the
presidential motorcade pass. They were at this location at 12:19 noon
when they were dispatched on the epileptic seizure call in the 100 block
North Houston Street. (D. Gurney & C. McSween, 2007)

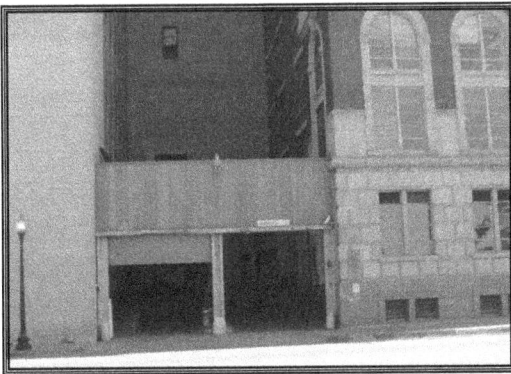

View of Sally-Port entrance of the Dallas County Jail directly across
from the epileptic seizure location.

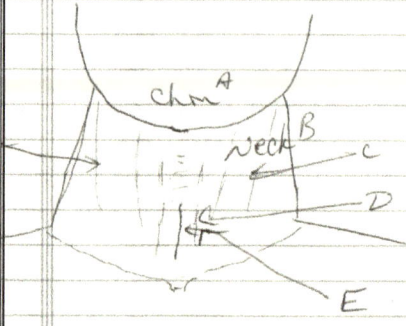

Anterior - Front Throat wound.

A - Chin
B - Neck
C - Prominence of
S.C.M Muscles
D - Prominence of
Trachea

E - 'Trach' cut
Running Vertically (Erect)

X Aubry Rike   Nov. 22, 2004
Aubrey Rike

witnessed X Alexia Rike

Aubrey's drawing of the wound he observed in Trauma Room 1 on President Kennedy's throat. "It appeared to me to be about an inch or maybe a bit more than that of a slit. With Kennedy's head tilted back on the stretcher, this caused me to think it ran vertically or lengthwise down the center of his throat..." The drawing indicates, " 'Trach' cut running vertically." (A. Rike & C. McSween, Nov.22, 2004)

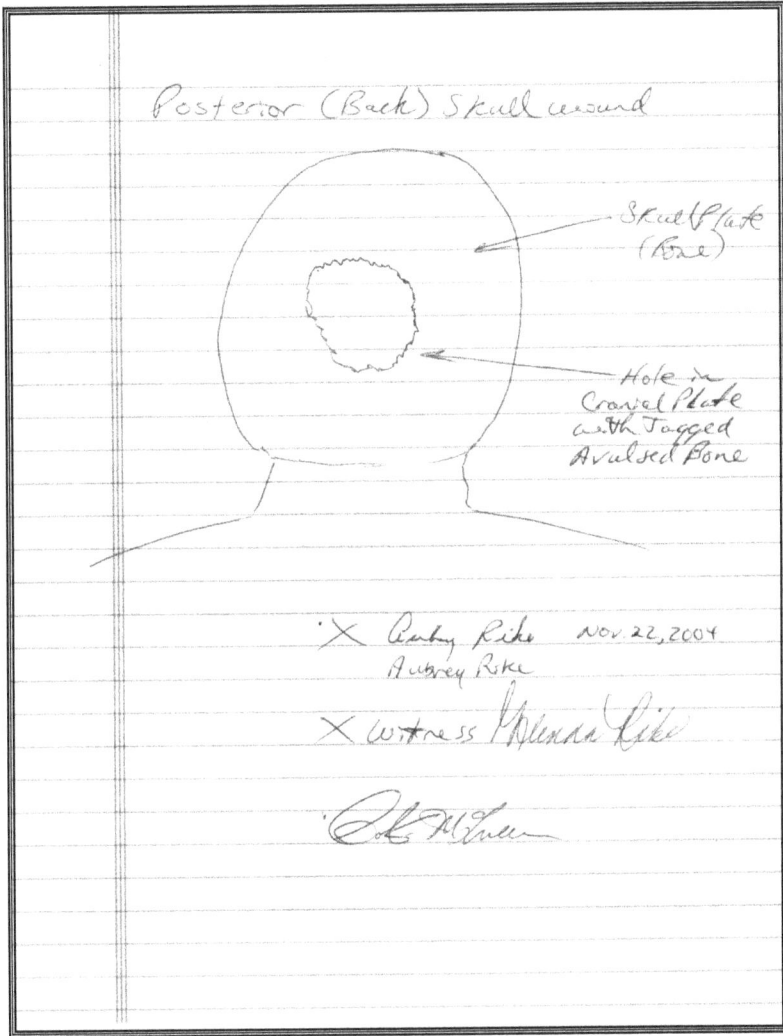

Aubrey's drawing of fatal wound in the back of President Kennedy's head which he felt with the palm of his hand while lifting the body. "I put my hand underneath his head...and I could feel that the skull had been blown out, blasted out. It had a jaggedy type feeling on my hand. It wasn't painful...but you could feel it, the edges of the bones through the sheet and on the palm of my hand....Also you could feel the President's brain. It felt like it was moving in my hand." (A. Rike & C. McSween, Nov.22, 2004)

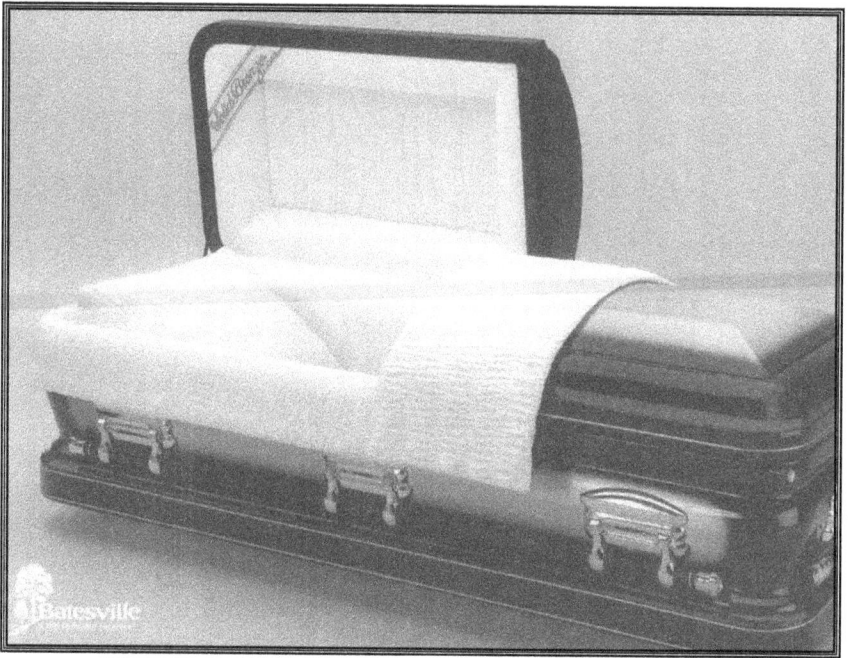

This solid bronze ceremonial casket is as close as is currently (2008) available in size, weight & design to the Elgin Britannia as provided by O'Neal Funeral Home in Dallas for the repatriation of President Kennedy." (C. McSween & Joe Weigel, Batesville Casket (C. McSween & Joe Weigel, Batesville Casket)

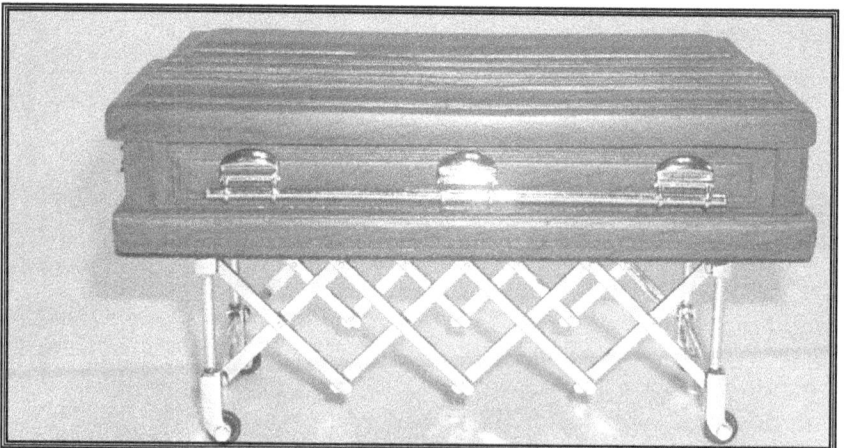

Model of casket on a folding Church Truck/casket dolly as used to wheel the bronze casket into and out of Parkland Memorial Hospital. (Chris @ C&R Collectibles, Langley, B.C.)

Interior rear compartment of hearse with Casket Table showing flush mounted rollers & head & foot pins for securing casket for transit. Mr. Oneal's hearse was had an attendant's jump seat on the extreme right side all the way forward nearer the passenger compartment partition.
(Chris @ C&R Collectibles, Langley, B.C.)

This lightweight utility grade aluminum shipping casket is what was described by members of the Navy Autopsy Staff at Bethesda Hospital as the type in which they received the body of President Kennedy.
(C. McSween, 1993)

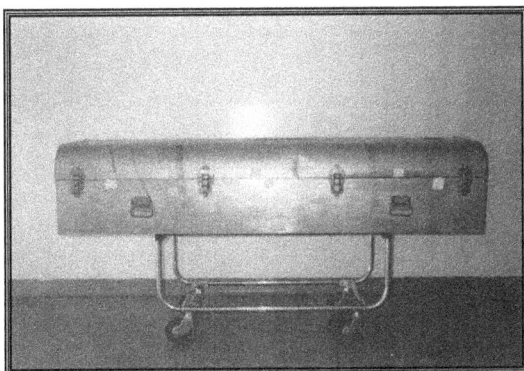

Aubrey Rike at the location in the 100 block of North Houston Street where he & Peanuts picked up the epileptic seizure patient at approximately 12:23 noon 11/22/1963. Note the Texas School Book Depository Building (TSBD) in the background. (C. McSween, 1993)

Appendix 2

The Parkland/Love Field/Air Force One Transfer

It has been long suggested that President Kennedy's body was intercepted or abducted and his wounds altered at some point between Parkland Memorial Hospital in Dallas, Texas and Bethesda Naval Hospital in Bethesda, Maryland.

There is stark contrast between what the Dallas doctors saw of the President's wounds at Parkland and what Paul O'Connor, James Jenkins, Floyd Reibe, Jerrol Custer and others saw at Bethesda. And those differnces are quite simply far too significant to ignore. The wounds as photographed at Bethesda bore little resemblance to the ones Aubrey observed and felt through the sheet that was wrapped around the President's head at Parkland.

It has been theorized that an interception of the President's body took place in Dallas. Removed from Parkland Memorial Hospital by one means or another, that the body was taken to O'Neal Funeral Home or to yet another destination and that the body never actually made it onto Air Force One at Love Field Airport at all.

It bears saying that the latter conjecture lacks some important consideration in so far as they missed interviewing one of the most critical witnesses to the event in question—Aubrey Rike.

The transfer of the body of President Kennedy from Parkland to Air force One was witnessed by Aubrey and his unwavering story has always been that the body was not altered prior to transfer onto Air Force One.

Aubrey Lee Rike is perhaps the only known witness alive at the time of this writing that can swear and attest that he:

1. Saw President Kennedy's mortal remains while in the presence of the widowed First Lady Jacqueline Kennedy, members of medical staff and the Secret Service.

2. Placed President Kennedy in the solid bronze casket and closed the lid.

3. Helped seal the casket lid.

4. Wheeled the casket from Trauma Room 1 out to the emergency area and to the rear compartment of Mr. O'Neal's hearse.

5. Placed the casket into the hearse.

6. Escorted the hearse directly to Love Field Airport without any route deviation, detour, or side trips.

7. Witnessed the bronze casket removed from Mr. O'Neal's hearse and placed on board Air Force One.

8. Witnessed the departure of Air Force One from Love Field Airport until it was air borne.

Appendix 3

Police Communication and Ambulance #606 Activity

Aubrey and Peanuts on duty in O'Neal ambulance #606 received their last routine dispatched call prior to the epileptic seizure call at a point in time between 10:30 and 11:00 AM (CST). They had cleared at 12:05 PM from this last trip from Baylor Hospital. By radioing themselves "Clear" they were in effect "Available" or were on "Stand-by" for another call.

The motorcade lead car—an unmarked police car —driven by Dallas Police Chief Jesse Curry whose police radio call sign was "One," was traveling immediately ahead of the presidential limousine. The lead vehicles were passing through Craddock Park and were about to pass beneath the Continental underpass on Lemmon Avenue near Lomo Alto.

The police communications went as follows.

> **Five:** *"Five to One."*
> **One:** *"Go ahead."*
> **Five:** *"What is your location now?"*
> **One:** *"One to Five."*
> **Five:** *"What is your location now?"*
> **One:** *"One to Five."*
> **Five:** *"What is your location now?"*
> **One:** *"We are approaching the Continental underpass near Lomo Alto."*
> **Dispatcher:**" *You read Five?"*
> **Five:** *"Ten-Four."*
> **Dispatcher:** *"Fifteen Car Two now on Lemmon nearing Lomo Alto. 12:05" [PM]*

From Lomo Alto the motorcade traveled another nine blocks before reaching the intersection of Lemmon Avenue and Oak Lawn Avenue. That intersection would be the closest the motorcade would pass to the location of the O'Neal Funeral Home. Aubrey and Peanuts were hoping to get back to the funeral home in time to see the presidential motorcade. Although some ten to twelve minutes behind schedule, the motorcade was making up for lost time and managed to pass the intersection at Oak Lawn within the next six minutes.

> **One:** *"One to Five Thirty One.*
> *One to Five Thirty*
> **One:** *Crossing Oak Lawn."*
> **Dispatcher**: *"Ten-Four One."*
> **One:** *"Okay Escort."*
> **Dispatcher:** *"Advise Three that the ambulances have arrived and are standing by. 12:11." [PM]*

In the minutes following this radio transmission, knowing that they would not be able to make it back to O'Neal's, Aubrey and Peanuts found a location at the south-east corner of Cedar Springs Road and Harwood Street where they could park their ambulance (#606) and watch the motorcade pass.

The last two-way radio transmission from Chief Curry prior to reaching the intersection of Cedar Springs and Harwood was:

> **One:** *"Cedar Springs and Fairmount."*
> **Dispatcher:** *"Ten-Four. 12:16...12:16." [PM]*

Fairmount was five blocks northeast of where Aubrey and Peanuts were parked at Cedar Springs and Harwood. The motorcade had picked up speed and easily closed this distance within the next two minutes. During this interval of time, Aubrey and Peanuts had climbed on top of their ambulance and were just in time to see President and Mrs.

Kennedy as their limousine made the left turn onto Harwood Street from Cedar Springs.

This left hand turn onto Harwood was made at approximately 12:18 p.m. as within the minute following, according to the FBI investigation, Aubrey and Peanuts were dispatched at 12:19 p.m. on the epileptic seizure call.

Immediately after exchanging enthusiastic waves with President Kennedy, Aubrey and Peanuts climbed down from the top of their ambulance just as the dispatch was coming over their radio [12:19 PM] on the epileptic seizure call which was located in the 100 block of North Houston Street in Dealey Plaza.

The next radio transmission from Chief Curry states:

> **One:** *"Harwood and McKinney."*
> **Dispatcher:** *"Harwood and McKinney*
> *fifteen car two. Ten-Four. Harwood*
> *and McKinney fifteen car two."*

McKinney is the first street that Harwood Street crosses when driving south from Cedar Springs Road. At this same point in time Aubrey and Peanuts were heading south on Pearl Street on code 3 heading for Main Street, on which they would turn right to go west to Houston Street for the epileptic patient.

Having received a heads-up that the crowd was significantly larger from Ross Avenue, which was another four blocks south on Harwood, Chief Curry stated the following:

> **One:** *"One to Five. I advise we got to try*
> *keep the crowd over about Harwood and Ross.*
> *We gotta get 'em out of the street there."*
> **Five:** *"We've got 'em."*
> **Dispatcher:** *"One are you approaching Ross?"*
> **One:** *"Just approaching it at this time."*
> **Dispatcher:** *"Ten-Four. 12:20."* [PM]

By about this same time Aubrey and Peanuts would have begun heading west on Main Street headed for Houston Street.

By 12:22 p.m. Chief Curry's lead car and the motorcade (still on Harwood) had traveled four blocks past Ross Avenue and had reached Live Oak Street.

> **One:** *"Just about to cross Live Oak."*
> **Five:** *"Ten-Four."*
> **Dispatcher:** *"12:22."* [PM]

From Live Oak the motorcade had three more blocks to travel before heading west on Main Street to Dealey Plaza. At this time Aubrey and Peanuts were involved with the epileptic seizure patient at Dealey Plaza.

Within 6 minutes of passing Live Oak the entire motorcade was on the Main street leg of the journey. At 12:26 PM the motorcade's lead car is crossing Field Street.

> **One:** *"Just at Field Street."*
> **Dispatcher:** *"Ten-Four. 12:26."* [PM]

By this time Aubrey and Peanuts were well on their way to Parkland Hospital with their Dealey Plaza patient.

At 12:28 PM the motorcade's lead car crosses Lamar Street.

> **One:** *"Crossing Lamar."*
> **Dispatcher:** *"Pretty good crowd there?"*
> **One:** *"Big crowd yes."*
> **Dispatcher:** *"Ten-Four. 12:28."* [PM]

Within the minute the lead car had reached Market Street and was only two short blocks from Houston Street and Dealey Plaza.

Dispatcher: *"Now on Main, probably just past Lamar."*
One: *"Just crossing Market Street."*
Dispatcher: *"Now at Market Car Two. 12:28." [PM]*

In the next two minutes the motorcade was well on its way through Dealey Plaza having turned right from Main Street into the 100 block of North Houston Street. From there the motorcade traveled north for one block before turning left into the 400 block of Elm Street. From there they would pass beneath The Triple Underpass before taking the ramp onto the Stemmons Freeway and to the Trade Mart beyond.

During this approximate interval of time Aubrey and Peanuts had unloaded their ambulance at Parkland Hospital and were in the process of wheeling their patient into the emergency department. Chief Curry gave his last pre-assassination two-way radio call while approaching the triple underpass with the motorcade.

One: *"Triple Underpass."*
Dispatcher: *"Ten-Four One. Fifteen Car Two. 12:30 KKB 364." [12:30 PM]*

The next call from Sheriff Decker, referred to as "Dallas One", came immediately after the shooting and included instructions to head to Parkland Hospital.

One (Curry): *"We're going to hospital officers! Go to hospital, we're on our way to Parkland Hospital, have them stand by! Get men up onto that underpass see what happened up there, go up to that overpass." One!...Have Parkland stand by!"*
Dallas One (Decker): *"One. Dallas One."*
Dispatcher: *"Go ahead Dallas One."*

Dallas One (Decker): *"I want my men and their material up on the railroad right-of-way there. I'm sure it's going to take some time to get your men in, I want all of my men in there."*
Dispatcher: *"Repeat One, I didn't quite understand all of it."*
Dallas One (Decker): *"Have Station Five (Decker's Office) remove all men available out of my department back there into the railroad yards there in an effort to try and determine in that block what happened in there and hold everything secure until a homicide and other investigators should get there."*
Dispatcher: *"Ten-Four Dallas One. Station Five read?"*
Dispatcher: *"One. Any information whatsoever?"*
One (Curry): *"Looks like the President's been hit. Have Parkland stand by!"*
Dispatcher: *"Ten-Four Parkland has been notified 12:32...notified."* [12:32 PM]

Within the next four minutes Chief Curry arrived at Parkland Hospital's emergency ambulance dock along with the presidential limousine, Secret Service car, vice-presidential car and his security detail and whomever else had managed to keep up to them.

Within another minute the Dallas Police had set up a perimeter of security around Parkland Hospital's emergency department.

125: *"We have the emergency entrance uh secured at Parkland."*
Dispatcher: *"Ten-Four One Twenty Five. 12:37."* [PM]

By approximately 12:42-12:43 PM President Kennedy was in Trauma Room 1 and major medical emergency efforts in an attempt to sustain his life were initiated.

The first official description of the suspected assassin went out over the Police radio at 12:45 PM. Within the next three minutes the Dallas Police were responding to information received on the epileptic incident with as much interest as they did to the details of the suspected shooter.

> **One:** *"We have an epileptic seizure just*
> *reported and he went to Parkland Hospital.*
> *See that the detectives downtown get all the*
> *information they can from this person."*
> **Dispatcher:** *"Ten-Four. 12:48."* [PM]

President Kennedy expired at 12:53 PM. Dr. Kemp Clark made the official pronouncement of President Kennedy's death as being at 1:00 PM (CST). Almost as soon as this a Secret Service agent had approached Aubrey and Peanuts asking if they were with a mortuary. Having established that they were, he asked them to contact their employer to bring a casket.

Upon this request Aubrey went to the telephone at the nursing desk in Major Medicine immediately adjacent to stall number eight where he had placed the epileptic seizure patient some 20 minutes earlier. While placing the call to Mr. O'Neal, Aubrey noticed that stall number eight was vacant and that the man had evidently left.

This treatment stall in Major Medicine was the last place Aubrey and Peanuts had seen the man. This was where they had transferred him from their ambulance gurney to the hospital gurney and where the Secret Service had taken charge of them to redress their gurney and be ready to transfer the President to St. Paul Hospital. The President's death had negated any need for a transfer to St. Paul.

So far as Aubrey is concerned the man that they had placed in stall number eight of Major Medicine had likely been moved out of the area at the orders of the FBI, Secret Service or by hospital administrative staff. No further information on the matter is available other than what is contained in the FBI documents of May 28, 1964, and June 11, 1964. Aubrey is satisfied with the findings of the FBI investigation as set forth in those documents.

Appendix 4

THE DALLAS CASKET & THE SHIPPING CASKET

In addressing the matter of the two different types of containers in question, the following definitions are placed here for the reader's convenient reference.

Dallas Casket = *Elgin Britannia solid bronze ceremonial* casket.
Shipping Casket = *Lightweight galvanized aluminum utility grade container.*

Much has been said pertaining to the matter of the casket that O'Neal Funeral Home provided for President Kennedy and into which Aubrey and Peanuts placed his body at Parkland Memorial Hospital in Dallas, Texas on November 22, 1963. That casket stands in evident contrast to the one reportedly received by autopsy personnel at the morgue that same evening at Bethesda Naval Hospital in Bethesda, Maryland.

One must have a reasonable, personal familiarity with these two very different funerary terms in order to have an appreciation for the vast differences that exist in these two very different caskets as pertains tit o the moving and transfer of the body of President Kennedy.

It bears a reminder to the reader that in this particular case, the terms "Ceremonial Casket" and "Shipping Casket" were not then and are not today simply two interchangeable terms used to pertain to the same item.

The matter of the casket provided for President Kennedy by O'Neal Funeral Home was addressed in some detail earlier in this book but it bears readdressing here. The casket that Mr. O'Neal placed in his 1964 Cadillac hearse and in which

Aubrey and Peanuts placed the body of President Kennedy was virtually a top-of-the-line casket by both 1963 and 2008 standards. It was manufactured by a casket company called the Elgin Casket Company and it was marketed as the "Elgin Britannia."

This casket was manufactured out of what is called in the metals industry solid sheet bronze. Bronze is deemed a Semi-Precious Metal and is marketed by reference to its' weight per square foot. This particular casket was manufactured out of forty-eight ounce bronze. This is three pounds per square foot of surface material. The finished product weighed four hundred pounds or somewhat heavier with the addition of items of hardware such as hinges, locks, handles, pivots, interior casket bed frame, etc. The quality of these caskets and the materials that go into making them cannot be overstated. Bronze is deemed a Semi-Precious Metal.

The manufacturing foundry process in which bronze is made is the result of a true refinery process involving the actual melting and blending of pure copper and pure zinc into one newly transformed substance. It is not merely a process of electroplating or galvanization. A 100% pure bronze metal is actually composed of 90% Copper and 10% Zinc.

In terms of color or routine factory process, copper on its own looks somewhat reddish-brown in color and all the more so when brushed. The addition of zinc to the copper creates two principal visual changes.

It causes the newly blended product—bronze—to appear gold in color. It causes the otherwise relatively soft characteristics of the copper to become hardened significantly and therefore far more durable.

Forty Eight (48) ounce solid bronze caskets were among the heaviest "Ceremonial" metal caskets commercially available in North America at that time and still are today without getting into the realm of "Custom" or "Special Orders". Of this 48 oz. weight category was the Elgin Britannia.

The Britannia casket was finished on the exterior in a deep brown shade or an oxidized patina finish that made it appear almost like a high quality exotic wood such as a mahogany. This latter type of finish is seldom seen in modern casket manufacture after about 1980.

The exterior was equipped with full length rail-type extension handles. The exterior also featured tapered and "urna" corners, which are the most expensive in casket manufacture due to the labor intensive process involved in manufacturing them. This also adds significantly to the appearance as well as to the dollar value of the product. The exterior of the Britannia also sported a glaze finish over the brown patina much like the final finishes applied to these types of caskets today. This type of finish tends to make the item look almost plastic in nature under certain lighting conditions. This latter point would account for the comment that Parkland Hospital's Head of Neurosurgery made in his summary notes that same afternoon when he described the casket that President Kennedy had left the hospital in as "…a bronze colored plastic casket…."

The Britannia casket exterior also featured domed, swell-top contoured lids with one-piece fishtail end panels that also contributed significantly to the product's dollar value. The Elgin Britannia's interior was finished in the finest white satin fabric available at the time. The bed itself was a fully adjustable and independent framed solid bronze body support fitted with metal slat styled springs and an upholstered dense foam mattress. The casket also featured a hermetic sealing system that was both air and watertight.

The O'Neal Funeral Home normally provided the Elgin Britannia casket with a complete funeral service for about $3000 in 1963. The Elgin Britannia solid bronze casket on it's own in 1963, had a retail value of from $2000 to $2500 without taking into consideration any additional cost of any other funeral services required or provided. Consider this in the age and economy of November 1963, when the minimum wage was $1.25 per hour.

The only known existing photos or film of the particular solid bronze casket were taken at Parkland Hospital's ambulance dock, being carried up the passenger ramp and onto Air Force One at Love Field Airport in Dallas, or when it was being off-loaded again at Andrew's Air Force Base after the flight home from Dallas to Washington, DC.

Most of these pieces of film were in black and white. In addition, the photos taken at Andrew's were taken after dark. Therefore, it follows that much of the detail of the casket is for the most part quite difficult to visually ascertain other than the fact that the casket looked very dark in any of the photographs or films available. For ease of clarification, we have provided a photograph in this book of the same type of casket provided by O'Neal Funeral Home for President Kennedy on Friday November 22, 1963.

Other than the exterior color, the solid bronze casket shown in this book is as close as any currently available in style and overall design (at the time of this writing-2008) to the Elgin Britannia bronze casket provided for the Dallas to Washington repatriation of President Kennedy's body.

There would be even more questions if the casket being off-loaded at Andrew's had been draped or wrapped in a casket flag as is most often the more current practice of the military when receiving their war dead home from a field of battle. However the Dallas casket was not draped in a flag and therefore quite a bit of the casket's exterior features may still be determined. Even a brief look by an untrained eye at those images of the Elgin Britannia solid bronze casket in contrast to a bare, unadorned and un-upholstered lightweight utility grade aluminum shipping casket will reveal the differences.

Strangely, although we see the images of the Dallas casket being off-loaded from Air Force One at Andrew's AFB, members of the morgue and autopsy staff at Bethesda Naval Hospital, including Paul Kelly O'Connor and James Curtis

Jenkins claimed repeatedly, over the course of some forty plus years, that what they received President Kennedy's body in at the morgue at Bethesda Naval Hospital the evening of Friday November 22, 1963, was a cheap shipping casket. Jenkins supported this claim.

Paul Kelly O'Connor is quoted as saying the casket was "a pinkish gray shipping casket, a light-weight aluminum shipping container weighing no more than 70 pounds when sitting empty."

In some cases, depending upon the manufacturer, shipping caskets are very basic metal utility cases and are often finished with a light, thin spray-on plastic type coating that aides in retarding the effects of oxidation. This coating also tends to make the exterior appear "pink" under certain types of lighting, especially many of the operating room type of lights used in many hospital morgues.

This type of casket or container is also known as a utilitarian container, or utility box, or in the forensic world and/or mortuary field we often refer to it as a "crash can" or a "floater tank" for reasons best left unsaid. Their interiors are essentially the same as what they are on the outside, a bare, unadorned, un-upholstered container with the most basic utility type handles or other hardware on the exterior. Any resemblance between a shipping casket and a ceremonial type casket such as an Elgin Britannia is an accident.

Unlike conventional ceremonial caskets, the lids of the utility shipping caskets or containers constitute almost one half of the overall container mass itself and the lids are unhinged. The lids, when on the container, are held on or secured in place by means of some six to eight basic metal clamps or clasps. When these clasps are undone, the entire lid simply lifts off to facilitate either placing the body into the container or for removing it.

This is the type of container that Paul O'Connor swore until the time of his death in August 2006, that he had removed

President Kennedy's body from at Bethesda Naval Hospital the evening of Friday November 22, 1963.

Paul O'Connor's account of the casket he lifted the President out of at the Bethesda morgue is most credible as in addition to being an attendant at the autopsy of President Kennedy, Paul had previously worked in the funeral service profession where he had frequent occasion to see all manner of ceremonial caskets as well as numerous shipping caskets.

Furthermore, in the years after the death of President Kennedy Paul had seen service in Vietnam in service in the medical corps where he saw several military aluminum shipping caskets on a routine basis. These caskets are what the military use when repatriating their war dead from a distant field of battle home to the United States. They generally look quite suitable as a casket in footage shown on television as in those instances they are most often completely draped or wrapped in a United States flag.

In October 1993, I hosted Paul O'Connor at a presentation we did together on the John F. Kennedy assassination at the college campus of Trinity Western University in Langley, British Columbia, Canada. For easy reference for Paul's use during his visual illustration, I had arranged with Imperial Casket Company of Burnaby, B. C. owner Gord Ropchan and his assistant Frank Scaglioni for some caskets to be on display. These caskets were placed on display stands alongside each other in a cluster. These were a Winchester Bronze casket which is as close as any available to the Elgin Britannia and a #710 Marsellus Solid African Mahogany Casket (as used for the formal Funeral Services and Burial of President Kennedy).

In addition to these two caskets, I had brought a third one from my own place of business—a lightweight aluminum utility grade shipping casket.

Paul O'Connor took a long carefull look at all three caskets, shook his head at the bronze casket, and said, "I never saw anything like this casket at Bethesda Naval Hospital that night of November 22, 1963, and certainly not with anything to do with President Kennedy. I would have remembered something as nice or well made as that."

Upon looking at the aluminum shipping casket Paul said, "This is basically what I remember seeing. This is what was placed on the morgue floor at Bethesda. We undid the clasps and removed the lid completely, unzipped the body bag and then lifted President Kennedy's body out of the container and placed him on the autopsy table."

For illustrative comparison purposes for the reader, this book contains photographs both of a solid bronze ceremonial casket as similar as currently available to that provided by O'Neal Funeral Home for President Kennedy in Dallas in November 1963. This book also contains a photograph of a basic utility grade aluminum shipping casket.

The specific aluminum shipping casket shown in this book is the exact same one that I had Paul O'Connor examine on a visit to my home in Canada one day while we were giving a presentation on the assassination. While inspecting the light-weight aluminum shipping casket with me, Paul said that this shipping casket was essentially identical to the one he had received President Kennedy's body in on the evening of Friday November 22, 1963, in the morgue at Bethesda Naval Hospital. He then immediately asked for photographs of the shipping casket that he could use in his presentations on the assassination.

Paul was with me later that same day and assisted me in unloading and replacing the casket back into inventory at the mortuary where I was employed at the time. As soon as Paul and I had unloaded the casket, I immediately took three photographs of the shipping casket in the basement of the mortuary where I was employed at the time.

The three photos shown in this book are those exact same three I took with my wife's camera while Paul O'Connor stood there with me. I then set about having a set of prints and slides made for Paul as well as an additional set made for David S. Lifton.

www.ingramcontent.com/pod-product-compliance
Lightning Source LLC
Chambersburg PA
CBHW020510100426
42813CB00030B/3188/J